PHILOSOPHY

THE BASICS

'*Philosophy: The Basics* deservedly remains the most recommended introduction to philosophy on the market. Warburton is patient, accurate and, above all, clear. There is no better short introduction to philosophy.'

Stephen Law, author of *The Philosophy Gym*

Philosophy: The Basics gently eases the reader into the world of philosophy. Each chapter considers a key area of philosophy, explaining and exploring the basic ideas and themes including:

- Can you prove God exists?
- How do we know right from wrong?
- How should we treat non-human animals?
- What are the limits of free speech?
- Do you know how science works?
- Is your mind different from your body?
- Can you define art?

For the fifth edition of this best-selling book, Nigel Warburton has added a new chapter on animals, revised others and brought the further reading sections up to date. If you've ever asked 'what is philosophy?', or wondered whether the world is really the way you think it is, this is the book for you.

Nigel Warburton is Senior Lecturer at The Open University. He is author of several books including *Philosophy: The Classics*, *Philosophy: Basic Readings*, *Thinking from A–Z*, and *The Basics of Essay Writing* all published by Routledge. He is co-creator, with David Edmonds, of the popular philosophy podcast *Philosophy Bites*.

The Basics

ACTING
BELLA MERLIN

ANTHROPOLOGY
PETER METCALF

ARCHAEOLOGY (SECOND EDITION)
CLIVE GAMBLE

ART HISTORY
GRANT POOKE AND DIANA NEWALL

ARTIFICIAL INTELLIGENCE
KEVIN WARWICK

THE BIBLE
JOHN BARTON

BUDDHISM
CATHY CANTWELL

CONTEMPORARY LITERATURE
SUMAN GUPTA

CRIMINAL LAW
JONATHAN HERRING

CRIMINOLOGY (SECOND EDITION)
SANDRA WALKLATE

DANCE STUDIES
JO BUTTERWORTH

EASTERN PHILOSOPHY
VICTORIA S. HARRISON

ECONOMICS (SECOND EDITION)
TONY CLEAVER

EDUCATION
KAY WOOD

EUROPEAN UNION (SECOND EDITION)
ALEX WARLEIGH-LACK

EVOLUTION
SHERRIE LYONS

FILM STUDIES
AMY VILLAREJO

FINANCE (SECOND EDITION)
ERIK BANKS

HUMAN GENETICS
RICKI LEWIS

HUMAN GEOGRAPHY
ANDREW JONES

INTERNATIONAL RELATIONS
PETER SUTCH AND JUANITA ELIAS

ISLAM (SECOND EDITION)
COLIN TURNER

JOURNALISM STUDIES
MARTIN CONBOY

JUDAISM
JACOB NEUSNER

LANGUAGE (SECOND EDITION)
R. L. TRASK

LAW
GARY SLAPPER AND DAVID KELLY

LITERARY THEORY (SECOND EDITION)
HANS BERTENS

LOGIC
J. C. BEALL

MANAGEMENT
MORGEN WITZEL

MARKETING (SECOND EDITION)
KARL MOORE AND NIKETH PAREEK

MEDIA STUDIES
JULIAN MCDOUGALL

THE OLYMPICS
ANDY MIAH AND BEATRIZ GARCIA

PHYSICAL GEOGRAPHY
JOSEPH HOLDEN

POETRY (SECOND EDITION)
JEFFREY WAINWRIGHT

POLITICS (FOURTH EDITION)
STEPHEN TANSEY AND NIGEL JACKSON

THE QUR'AN
MASSIMO CAMPANINI

RACE AND ETHNICITY
PETER KIVISTO AND PAUL R. CROLL

RELIGION (SECOND EDITION)
MALORY NYE

RELIGION AND SCIENCE
PHILIP CLAYTON

RESEARCH METHODS
NICHOLAS WALLIMAN

ROMAN CATHOLICISM
MICHAEL WALSH

SEMIOTICS (SECOND EDITION)
DANIEL CHANDLER

SHAKESPEARE (THIRD EDITION)
SEAN MCEVOY

SOCIAL WORK
MARK DOEL

SOCIOLOGY
KEN PLUMMER

SPECIAL EDUCATIONAL NEEDS
JANICE WEARMOUTH

TELEVISION STUDIES
TOBY MILLER

TERRORISM
JAMES LUTZ AND BRENDA LUTZ

THEATRE STUDIES
ROBERT LEACH

WORLD HISTORY
PETER N. STEARNS

PHILOSOPHY

THE BASICS

FIFTH EDITION

Nigel Warburton

Routledge
Taylor & Francis Group

LONDON AND NEW YORK

First edition published 1992
Second edition published 1995
Third edition published 1999
Fourth edition published 2004
Fifth edition published 2013
by Routledge
2 Park Square, Milton Park, Abingdon, Oxon OX14 4RN

Simultaneously published in the USA and Canada
by Routledge
711 Third Avenue, New York, NY 10017

Routledge is an imprint of the Taylor & Francis Group, an informa business

British Library Cataloguing in Publication Data
A catalogue record for this book is available from the British Library

Library of Congress Cataloging in Publication Data
Warburton, Nigel, 1962-
Philosophy : the basics / Nigel Warburton. -- 5th ed.
p. cm.
Includes bibliographical references (p.) and index.
1. Philosophy--Introductions. I. Title.
BD21.W35 2012
100--dc23
2012006466

ISBN: 978-0-415-69317-2 (hbk)
ISBN: 978-0-415-69316-5 (pbk)

Typeset in Bembo and Scala Sans
by Taylor & Francis Books
Printed and bound by CPI Group (UK) Ltd, Croydon, CR0 4YY

For my mother

CONTENTS

PREFACE

For this fifth edition I have added a new short chapter, 'Animals', and have made minor corrections and additions throughout. I have also brought the further reading up to date and have created webpages at www.philosophythebasics.com with links to relevant online resources including podcasts.

I would like to thank all those who commented on drafts of various chapters or helped in other ways. In particular, I am grateful to Alexandra Alexandri, Gunnar Arnason, Jennifer Burgess, Inga Burrows, Eric Butcher, Michael Camille, Simon Christmas, Lesley Cohen, Emma Cotter, Tim Crane, Sue Derry-Penz, Angie Doran, Adrian Driscoll, David Edmonds, Goober Fox, Jonathan Hourigan, Rosalind Hursthouse, Paul Jefferis, Maria Kasmirli, John Kimbell, Stephen Law, Robin Le Poidevin, Georgia Mason, Hugh Mellor, Alex Miller, Anna Motz, Penny Nettle, Alex Orenstein, Andrew Pyle, Abigail Reed, Anita Roy, Ron Santoni, Helen Simms, Jennifer Trusted, Phillip Vasili, Stephanie Warburton, Tessa Watt, Jonathan Wolff, Kira Zurawska, and the publisher's anonymous readers.

Nigel Warburton
Oxford 2012
www.nigelwarburton.com
www.virtualphilosopher.com
www.philosophybites.com
www.twitter.com/philosophybites

INTRODUCTION

What is philosophy? This is a notoriously difficult question. One of the easiest ways of answering it is to say that philosophy is what philosophers do, and then point to the writings of Plato, Aristotle, Descartes, Hume, Kant, Russell, Wittgenstein, Sartre, and other famous philosophers. However, this answer is unlikely to be of much use to you if you are just beginning the subject, as you probably won't have read anything by these writers. Even if you have, it may still be difficult to say what they have in common, if indeed there is a relevant characteristic which they all share. Another approach to the question is to point out that philosophy is derived from the Greek word meaning 'love of wisdom'. However, this is rather vague and even less helpful than saying that philosophy is what philosophers do. So some very general comments about what philosophy is are needed.

Philosophy is an activity: it is a way of thinking about certain sorts of question. Its most distinctive feature is its use of logical argument. Philosophers typically deal in arguments: they either invent them, criticize other people's, or do both. They also analyse and clarify concepts. The word 'philosophy' is often used in a much broader sense than this to mean one's general outlook on life, or else to refer to some forms of mysticism. I will not be using the word in this broader sense here: my aim is to illuminate some of the key areas of discussion in a tradition of thought which began with the Ancient Greeks and flourished in the twentieth century, predominantly in Europe, North America, Australia, and New Zealand. This tradition looks set to continue well into the present century.

What kind of things do philosophers working in this tradition argue about? They often examine beliefs that most of us take for granted most of the time. They are concerned with questions about what could loosely be called 'the meaning of life': questions about religion, right and wrong, politics, the nature of reality, the mind, science, art, and numerous other topics. For instance, most people live their lives without questioning their fundamental beliefs, such as that killing is wrong. But why is it wrong? What justification is there for saying that killing is wrong? Is it wrong in every circumstance? What about killing in self-defence? What about killing animals painlessly? And what do I mean by 'wrong' anyway? These are philosophical questions. Many of our beliefs, when examined, turn out to have firm foundations, but some do not. The study of philosophy not only helps us to think clearly about our prejudices, but also helps to clarify precisely what we do believe. In the process it develops an ability to argue coherently on a wide range of issues – a useful transferable skill.

PHILOSOPHY AND ITS HISTORY

Since the time of Socrates there have been many great philosophers. I named a few of these in my opening paragraph. An introductory book on philosophy could approach the subject historically, analysing the contributions of these philosophers in chronological order. This is not what I shall do here. Instead I will use a topic-based approach: one focusing on particular philosophical questions rather than on history. The history of philosophy is a fascinating and important subject in its own right, and many of the classic philosophical texts are also great works of literature: Plato's Socratic dialogues, René Descartes's *Meditations*, David Hume's *Enquiry Concerning Human Understanding*, and Friedrich Nietzsche's *Thus Spake Zarathustra*, to take just a few examples, all stand out as compelling pieces of writing by any standards. Whilst there is great value in the study of the history of philosophy, my aim here is to give you the tools to think about philosophical issues yourselves rather than simply to explain what certain great figures have thought about them. These issues are not just of interest to philosophers: they arise naturally out of the human situation and many people who have never opened a philosophy book spontaneously think about them.

Any serious study of philosophy will involve a mixture of historical and topic-based study, since if we don't know about the arguments and errors of earlier philosophers, we cannot hope to make a substantial contribution to the subject. Without some knowledge of history philosophers would never progress: they would keep making the same mistakes, unaware that they had been made before. And many philosophers develop their own theories by seeing what is wrong with the work of earlier philosophers. However, in a short book such as this it is impossible to do justice to the complexities of individual thinkers' work. The further reading suggested at the end of each chapter should help to put the issues discussed here into a broader historical context.

WHY STUDY PHILOSOPHY?

It is sometimes argued that there is no point in studying philosophy as all philosophers ever do is sit around quibbling over the meaning of words. They never seem to reach any conclusions of any impor-tance and their contribution to society is virtually non-existent. They are still arguing about the same problems that interested the Ancient Greeks. Philosophy does not seem to change anything; philosophy leaves everything as it is.

What is the value of studying philosophy at all? Starting to question the fundamental assumptions of our lives could even be dangerous: we might end up feeling unable to do anything, paralysed by questioning too much. Indeed, the caricature of a philosopher is of someone who is brilliant at dealing with very abstract thought in the comfort of an armchair in an Oxford or Cambridge common room, but is hopeless at dealing with the practicalities of life: someone who can explain the most complicated passages of Hegel's philosophy, but can't work out how to boil an egg.

THE EXAMINED LIFE

One important reason for studying philosophy is that it deals with fundamental questions about the meaning of our existence. Most of us at some time in our lives ask ourselves basic philosophical questions. Why are we here? Is there any proof that God exists? Is there any purpose to our lives? What makes anything right or wrong? Could we ever be justified in breaking the law? Could our lives be just a dream? Is mind different from body, or are we simply physical beings? How does science progress? Do animals have rights? What is art? And so on.

Most people who study philosophy believe that it is important that each of us examines such questions. Some even argue that an unexamined life is not worth living. To carry on a routine existence without ever examining the principles on which it is based may be like driving a car which has never been serviced. You may be justified in trusting the brakes, the steering, the engine, since they have always worked well enough up until now; but you may be completely unjustified in this trust: the brake pads may be faulty and fail you when you most need them. Similarly the principles on which your life is based may be entirely sound, but until you've examined them, you can't be certain of this.

However, even if you do not seriously doubt the soundness of the assumptions on which your life is based, you may be impoverishing your life by not exercising your power of thought. Many people find it either too much of an effort or too disturbing to ask themselves such fundamental questions: they may be happy and comfortable with their prejudices. But others have a strong desire to find answers to challenging philosophical questions.

LEARNING TO THINK

Another reason for studying philosophy is that it provides a good way of learning to think more clearly about a wide range of issues. The methods of philosophical thought can be useful in a variety of situations, since by analysing the arguments for and against any position and coming to a conclusion we learn skills which can be transferred to other areas of life. Many people who study philosophy go on to apply their philosophical skills in jobs as diverse as the law, computer programming, management consultancy, the civil service, and journalism – all areas in which clarity of thought is a great asset. Philosophers also use the insights they gain about the nature of human existence when they turn to the arts: a number of philosophers have also been successful as novelists, critics, poets, film-makers, and playwrights.

PLEASURE

A further justification for the study of philosophy is that for many people it can be a very pleasurable activity. There is something to be said for this defence of philosophy. Its danger is that it could be taken to be reducing philosophical activity to the equivalent of solving crossword puzzles. At times some philosophers' approach to the subject can seem very like this: some professional philosophers become obsessed with solving obscure logical puzzles as an end in itself, publishing their solutions in esoteric journals. At another extreme, some philosophers working in universities see themselves as part of a 'business', and publish what is often mediocre work simply because it will allow them to 'get on' and achieve promotion (quantity of publications being a factor in determining who is promoted). They experience pleasure from seeing their name in print, and from the increased salary and prestige that go with promotion. Fortunately, however, much philosophy rises above this level.

IS PHILOSOPHY DIFFICULT?

Philosophy is often described as a difficult subject. There are various kinds of difficulty associated with it, some avoidable.

It is true that many of the problems with which professional philosophers deal do require quite a high level of abstract thought. However, the same is true of almost any intellectual pursuit: philosophy is no different in this respect from physics, literary criticism, computer programming, geology, mathematics, or history. As with these and other areas of study, the difficulty of making substantial original contributions to the subject should not be used as an excuse for denying ordinary people knowledge of advances made in it, or for preventing them learning their basic methods.

However, there is a second kind of difficulty associated with philosophy which can be avoided. Philosophers are not always good writers. Many of them are extremely poor communicators of their ideas. Sometimes this is because they are only interested in reaching a very small audience of specialist readers; sometimes it is because they use unnecessarily complicated jargon which simply confuses those unfamiliar with it. Specialist terms can be helpful, to avoid having to explain particular concepts every time they are used. However, among professional philosophers there is an unfortunate tendency to use specialist terms for their own sake; many of them use Latin phrases even though there are perfectly good English equivalents. A paragraph peppered with unfamiliar words and familiar words used in unfamiliar ways can be intimidating. Some philosophers seem to speak and write in a language they have invented themselves. This can make philosophy appear to be a much more difficult subject than it really is. It can be a smokescreen behind which second-rate philosophers hide.

In this book I have tried to avoid unnecessary jargon and have explained all unfamiliar terms as I go along. This approach should give you the basic philosophical vocabulary needed for understanding some of the more difficult philosophical writing recommended in the reading lists at the end of each chapter.

THE LIMITS OF WHAT PHILOSOPHY CAN DO

Some students of philosophy have unreasonably high expectations of the subject. They expect it to provide them with a complete and detailed picture of the human predicament. They think that philosophy will reveal to them the meaning of life, and explain to them every facet of our complex existences. Now, although studying philosophy can illuminate fundamental questions about our lives, it does not provide anything like a complete picture, if indeed there could be such a thing. Studying philosophy isn't an alternative to studying art, literature, history, psychology, anthropology, sociology, politics, and science. These different subjects concentrate on different aspects of human life and provide different sorts of insight. Some aspects of anyone's life will defy philosophical analysis, and perhaps analysis of any other kind too. It is important, then, not to expect too much of philosophy.

HOW TO USE THIS BOOK

I have already stressed that philosophy is an activity. So this book should not be read passively. It would be possible simply to learn the arguments used here by heart, but that alone would not be learning to philosophize, though it would provide a sound knowledge of many of the basic arguments philosophers use. The ideal reader of this book will read it critically, constantly questioning the arguments used, and thinking of counter-arguments. This book is intended to stimulate thought, not to be an alternative to it. If you read it critically you will no doubt find much with which you disagree and in the process you will clarify your own beliefs.

Although I have tried to make all the chapters accessible to someone who has never studied philosophy before, some are more difficult than others. Most people have at least considered the question of whether or not God exists, and have considered the arguments on either side – consequently the chapter on God should be relatively easy to follow. On the other hand, few non-philosophers will have thought in detail about some of the topics addressed in the chapters on reality, on the mind, and in the more abstract sections of the chapter on right and wrong. These chapters, particularly the one on the mind, may take longer to read. I recommend that you skim over the chapters to begin with, then go back to specific parts which you find interesting, rather than working slowly through section by section, risking becoming swamped in the detail without having a sense of how the different arguments relate to each other.

There is one obvious topic which this book might have included but doesn't: logic. I have left this out because it is too technical an area to be dealt with satisfactorily in a book of this length and style.

Students should find this book useful to consolidate what they learn in lectures, and as an aid to essay-writing: I give a summary of the main philosophical approaches to each topic, together with a number of criticisms of them. This can easily be plundered for ideas for essays.

FURTHER READING

A collection of articles and extracts, *Philosophy: Basic Readings* (2nd edition, London: Routledge, 2004) complements this book. It follows the same structure as *Philosophy: The Basics*. *Western Philosophy: An Anthology*, edited by John Cottingham (Oxford: Blackwell, 1996), is a more historically orientated selection of readings.

Thomas Nagel's *What Does It All Mean?* (Oxford: Oxford University Press, 1987) is a good brief introduction to philosophy.

Stephen Law's *The Philosophy Gym: 25 Short Adventures in Thinking* (London: Review, 2003) is an interesting and lively introduction to the subject which makes use of dialogues and stories as well as more conventional exposition. Two other books by the same author, though written for young teenagers, are also excellent: *The Philosophy Files* (London: Orion, 2002 – this has been published as *Philosophy Rocks* in the US) and *The Outer Limits* (London: Orion, 2003). Simon Blackburn's *Think* (Oxford: Oxford University Press, 2001) is considerably more difficult in places, but well worth reading. Bryan Magee's *The Great Philosophers* (Oxford: Oxford University Press, 1987) is a good introduction to the history of philosophy. It consists of conversations with a number of present-day philosophers about great philosophers of the past and is based on the BBC television series of the same name. My book *Philosophy: The Classics* (3rd edition, Abingdon: Routledge, 2006) focuses on twenty-seven key books by philosophers, from Plato's *Republic* to Rawls's *A Theory of Justice*. Edward Craig's *Philosophy: A Very Short Introduction* (Oxford: Oxford University Press, 2002) also introduces philosophy through some classic works.

A Dictionary of Philosophy, edited by Antony Flew (London: Pan, 1979), is useful for reference, as is A. R. Lacey's *A Dictionary of Philosophy* (London: Routledge, 1976). *The Blackwell Companion to Philosophy*, edited by Nicholas Bunnin and E. P. Tsui-James (Oxford: Blackwell, 1996), provides useful introductions to the central areas of philosophy and to a selection of major thinkers. If you have access to a good library, *The Routledge Encyclopedia of Philosophy*, edited by Edward Craig (London: Routledge, 1998), is certainly worth consulting. It provides detailed and up-to-date entries on all the central topics within philosophy.

Think, edited by Stephen Law, and published three times a year, is the Royal Institute of Philosophy's journal. It is accessible and interesting and contains articles on a very wide range of topics; further details are available from www.royalinstitutephilosophy.org/think. *The Philosophers' Magazine* is another important publication for anyone interested in philosophy. Further details of this are available from www.philosophers.co.uk. The magazine *Philosophy Now* has a website at www.philosophynow.org. For those interested in methods of argument used by philosophers there are a number of relevant books including my own *Thinking from A to Z* (3rd edition,

London: Routledge, 2007), Anthony Weston's *A Rulebook for Arguments* (2nd edition, Indianapolis, Ind.: Hackett, 2001), Anne Thomson's *Critical Reasoning* (2nd edition, London: Routledge, 2001), and Alec Fisher's *Critical Thinking: An Introduction* (Cambridge: Cambridge University Press, 2001). Michael Clark's *Paradoxes from A to Z* (London: Routledge, 2002) is also very good. My own *Philosophy: The Essential Study Guide* (London: Routledge, 2004) introduces the basic study skills in philosophy.

On the topic of writing clearly, and why it is important, George Orwell's essay 'Politics and the English Language', which is in *The Penguin Essays of George Orwell* (London: Penguin, 1990), is well worth reading. For practical advice in this area, try Ernest Gowers's *The Complete Plain Words* (London: Penguin, 1962) and *Plain English* by Diané Collinson, Gillian Kirkup, Robin Kyd, and Lynne Slocombe (2nd edition, Milton Keynes: Open University Press, 1992). My own book *The Basics of Essay Writing* (Abingdon: Routledge, 2006) is a general introduction to writing in the Humanities.

INTERNET RESOURCES

There are now numerous excellent online philosophy resources, including podcasts and videos. I have linked to a range of these from the pages at www.philosophythebasics.com. You can also follow me on Twitter at www.twitter.com/philosophybites for links to philosophically interesting online material.

1

GOD

Does God exist? This is a fundamental question, one which most of us ask ourselves at some time in our lives. The answer which each of us gives affects not only the way we behave, but also how we understand and interpret the world, and what we expect for the future. If God exists, then human existence may have a purpose, and we may even hope for eternal life. If not, then we must create any meaning in our lives for ourselves: no meaning will be given to them from outside, and death is probably final.

When philosophers turn their attention to religion they typically examine the various arguments that have been given for and against God's existence. They weigh up the evidence and look closely at the structure and implications of the arguments. They also examine concepts such as faith and religious belief to see if they can make sense of the way people talk about God.

The starting point for most philosophy of religion is a very general doctrine about the nature of God, known as Theism. This is the view that one God exists, that he or she is omnipotent (capable of doing anything), omniscient (knows everything), and supremely benevolent (all-good). Such a view is held by most Christians, Jews, and Muslims alike. Here I will focus on the Christian view of God, though most of the arguments will apply equally to the other Theistic religions, and some will be relevant to any religion.

But does this God described by Theists actually exist? Can we prove that he or she does? Should a reasonable person believe that no such God exists, a position known as atheism? Or is agnosticism, the suspension of belief (or sitting on the fence, as some people would describe it), the appropriate reaction? There are many different arguments intended to prove God's existence. I shall consider the most important of these in this chapter.

THE DESIGN ARGUMENT

One of the most frequently used arguments for God's existence is the Design Argument, sometimes also known as the Teleological Argument (from the Greek word *telos*, which means 'purpose'). This states that if we look around us at the natural world we can't help noticing how everything in it is suited to the function it performs: everything bears evidence of having been designed. This is supposed to demonstrate the existence of a Creator. If, for example, we examine the human eye, we see how its minute parts all fit together, each part cleverly suited to what it was apparently made for: seeing.

Supporters of the Design Argument, such as William Paley (1743–1805), claim that the complexity and efficiency of natural objects such as the eye are evidence that they must have been designed by God. How else could they have come to be as they are? Just as by looking at a watch we can tell that it was designed by a watchmaker, so, they argue, we can tell by looking at the eye that it was designed by some sort of Divine Watchmaker. It is as if God has deliberately left evidence of his or her existence all around us in the world.

This is an argument from an effect to its cause: we look at the effect (the watch or the eye), and from examination of it we try to tell what caused it (a watchmaker or a Divine Watchmaker). It relies on the idea that a designed object like a watch is in some ways very similar to a natural object such as the eye. This sort of argument, based on a similarity between two things, is known as an argument from analogy. Arguments from analogy rely on the principle that if two things are similar in some respects they will very likely be similar in others.

Those who accept the Design Argument tell us that everywhere we look, particularly in the natural world – whether at trees, cliffs, animals, the stars, or whatever – we can find further confirmation of God's existence. Because these things are far more ingeniously constructed than a watch, the Divine Watchmaker must have been correspondingly more intelligent than the human watchmaker. Indeed, the Divine Watchmaker must have been so powerful, and so clever, that it makes sense to assume that it was God as traditionally understood by Theists.

However, there are strong arguments against the Design Argument, several of which were raised by the philosopher David Hume (1711–76) in his posthumously published *Dialogues Concerning Natural Religion*, and in section XI of his *Enquiry Concerning Human Understanding*.

CRITICISMS OF THE DESIGN ARGUMENT

WEAKNESS OF ANALOGY

One objection to the argument just set forth is that it relies on a weak analogy: it takes for granted that there is a significant resemblance between natural objects and objects which we know to have been designed. But it is not obvious that, to use the same example again, the human eye really is like a watch in any important respect. Arguments from analogy rely on there being a strong similarity between the two things being compared. If the similarity is weak, then the conclusions that can be drawn on the basis of the comparison are correspondingly weak. So, for example, a wrist watch and a pocket watch are sufficiently similar for us to be able to assume that they were both designed by watchmakers. But although there is some similarity between a watch and an eye – they are both intricate and fulfil their particular functions – it is only a vague similarity, and any conclusions based on the analogy will as a result be correspondingly vague.

Against this criticism a Theist might still maintain that it is more likely that the eye was designed by a supreme being than that it came about merely by chance.

EVOLUTION

The existence of a Divine Watchmaker is not, however, the only possible explanation of how it is that animals and plants are so well adapted to their functions. In particular, Charles Darwin's (1809–82) theory of evolution by natural selection, explained in his book *The Origin of Species* (1859), gives a widely accepted alternative explanation of this phenomenon. Darwin showed how, by a process of the survival of the fittest, those animals and plants best suited to their environments lived to pass on their characteristics to their offspring. Later scientists have been able to account for the mechanism of evolution in terms of inherited genes. This process explains how such marvellous adaptations to environment as are found in the animal and plant kingdoms could have occurred, without needing to introduce the notion of God.

Of course Darwin's theory of evolution in no way *disproves* God's existence – indeed, many Christians accept it as the best explanation of how plants, animals, and human beings came to be as they are: they believe that God created the mechanism of evolution itself. However, Darwin's theory does weaken the power of the Design Argument since it explains the same effects without any mention of God as their cause. The existence of such a theory about the mechanism of biological adaptation prevents the Design Argument from being a conclusive proof of God's existence.

LIMITATIONS ON CONCLUSION

Even if, despite the objections mentioned so far, you still find the Design Argument convincing, you should notice that it doesn't prove the existence of a unique, all-powerful, all-knowing, and all-good God. Close examination of the argument shows it to be limited in a number of ways.

First, the argument completely fails to support monotheism – the view that there is just one God. Even if you accept that the world and everything in it clearly shows evidence of having been designed, there is no reason to believe that it was all designed by one God. Why couldn't it have been designed by a team of lesser gods working together? After all, most large-scale, complex human constructions such as skyscrapers, pyramids, space rockets, and so on, were made by teams of individuals, so surely if we carry the analogy to its logical conclusion it will lead us to believe that the world was designed by a group of gods working together.

Second, the argument doesn't necessarily support the view that the Designer (or designers) was all-powerful. It could plausibly be argued that the universe has a number of 'design faults': for instance, the human eye has a tendency to short-sightedness, and to cataracts in old age – hardly the work of an all-powerful Creator wanting to create the best world possible. Such observations might lead some people to think that the Designer of the universe, far from being all-powerful, was a comparatively weak god or gods, or possibly a young god experimenting with his or her powers. Maybe the Designer died soon after creating the universe, allowing it to run down of its own accord. The Design Argument provides at least as much evidence for these conclusions as it does for the existence of the God described by the Theists. So the Design Argument alone cannot prove that the Theists' God rather than some other type of God or gods exists.

Finally, on the question of whether the Designer is all-knowing and all-good, many people find the amount of evil in the world counts against this conclusion. This evil ranges from human cruelty, murder, and torture, to the suffering caused by natural disasters and disease. If, as the Design Argument suggests, we are to look around us to see the evidence of God's work, many people will find it hard to accept that what they see is the result of a benevolent Creator. An all-knowing God would know that evil exists; an all-powerful God would be able to prevent it occurring; and an all-good God would not want it to exist. But evil continues to occur. This serious challenge to belief in the Theists' God has been much discussed by philosophers. It is known as the Problem of Evil. In a later section we will examine it in some detail, together with several attempted solutions to it. Here it should at least make us wary about claims that the Design Argument provides conclusive evidence for the existence of a supremely good God.

As can be seen from this discussion, the Design Argument can only give us, at best, the very limited conclusion that the world and everything in it was designed by something or someone. To go beyond this would be to overstep what can logically be concluded from the argument.

THE FINE TUNING ARGUMENT

Despite the powerful arguments against the Design Argument, some recent thinkers have tried to defend a variant of it known as the Anthropic Principle. This is the view that the chance of the world turning out to be conducive to human survival and development was so tiny that we can conclude that the world is the work of a divine architect. On this view, the fact that human beings have evolved and survived provides us with a proof of God's existence. God must have controlled the physical conditions in our universe, and fine-tuned them to allow just this kind of life form to evolve. This view is bolstered by scientific research indicating the limited range of suitable starting conditions for a universe in which life could develop at all.

CRITICISM OF THE FINE TUNING ARGUMENT

THE LOTTERY OBJECTION

There is a major objection to the argument from Fine Tuning. Imagine that you have bought a ticket for a national lottery. There are, perhaps, many millions of tickets, but only one will win. It is statistically highly unlikely that you will win. But you might. If you do, however, this doesn't demonstrate more than your good luck: it doesn't follow from the fact that, from amongst all those millions of losing tickets, your winning ticket was chosen that this must have been the result of something more than a random selection. You might, if you are superstitious, read all kinds of significance into the fact that you won the lottery. But anything which is statistically unlikely still can happen. The mistake that defenders of the Fine Tuning argument make is to assume that when something happens which is unlikely, there must be a more plausible explanation of it than that it arose naturally. Our presence in this part of the universe can be adequately explained without recourse to supernatural causes. It is not surprising that we are in a universe where the conditions were just right for beings of our kind to emerge, since there would be no chance whatsoever of us emerging elsewhere. So the fact that we are here cannot be taken as proof of God's design. Furthermore, the Fine Tuning argument is also vulnerable to the range of criticisms of traditional versions of the Design Argument outlined above.

THE FIRST CAUSE ARGUMENT

The Design Argument and its variant the Fine Tuning Argument are based on direct observation of the world. As such they are what philosophers call empirical arguments. In contrast, the First Cause Argument, sometimes known as the Cosmological Argument, relies only on the empirical fact that the universe exists, not on any particular facts about what it is like.

The First Cause Argument states that absolutely everything has been caused by something else prior to it: nothing has just sprung into existence without a cause. Because we know that the universe exists, we can safely assume that a whole series of causes and effects led to its being as it is. If we follow this series back we will find an original cause, the very first cause. This first cause, so the First Cause Argument tells us, is God.

However, as with the Design Argument, there are a number of criticisms of this argument.

CRITICISMS OF THE FIRST CAUSE ARGUMENT

SELF-CONTRADICTORY

The First Cause Argument begins with the assumption that every single thing was caused by something else, but it then proceeds to contradict this by saying that God was the very first cause. It argues both that there can be no uncaused cause, and that there is one uncaused cause: God. It invites the question 'And what caused God?' Someone convinced by the First Cause Argument might object that they did not mean that *everything* had a cause, only that everything except God had a cause. But this is no better. If the series of effects and causes is going to stop somewhere, why must it stop at God? Why couldn't it stop earlier in the regression, with the appearance of the universe itself?

NOT A PROOF

The First Cause Argument assumes that effects and causes could not possibly go back for ever in what is termed an infinite regress: a never-ending series going back in time. It assumes that there was a first cause that gave rise to all other things. But must this really have been so?

If we used a similar argument about the future, then we would suppose that there would be some final effect, one which would not be the cause of anything after it. But, although it is indeed difficult to imagine, it does seem plausible to think of causes and effects going on into the future to infinity, just as there is no highest number because we can always add one to any number which is supposed to be the highest one. If it is possible to have an infinite series at all, why then shouldn't the effects and causes extend backwards into the past to infinity?

LIMITATIONS ON CONCLUSION

Even if these two criticisms of the argument can be met, it does not prove that the first cause is the God described by the Theists. As with the Design Argument, there are serious limitations on what can be concluded from the First Cause Argument.

First, it is true that the first cause was probably extremely powerful in order to create and set in motion the series of causes and effects which resulted in the whole universe as we now know it. So there might be some justification for claiming that the argument shows the existence of a very powerful, if not an all-powerful, God.

But the argument presents no evidence whatsoever for a God who is either all-knowing or all-good. Neither of these attributes would be needed by a first cause. And, as with the Design Argument, a defender of the First Cause Argument would still be left with the problem of how an all-powerful, all-knowing, and all-good God could tolerate the amount of evil that there is in the world.

THE ONTOLOGICAL ARGUMENT

The Ontological Argument is very different from the previous two arguments for the existence of God in that it does not rely on evidence at all. The Design Argument, as we have seen, depends on evidence about the nature of the world and the objects and organisms in it; the First Cause Argument requires less evidence – it is based only on the observation that something rather than nothing exists. The Ontological Argument, however, is an attempt to show that the existence of God necessarily follows from the definition of God as the supreme being. Because this conclusion can be drawn *prior* to experience, it is known as an *a priori* argument.

According to the Ontological Argument, God is defined as the most perfect being imaginable; or, in the most famous formulation of the argument, given by St Anselm (1033–1109), as 'that being than which nothing greater can be conceived'. One of the aspects of this perfection or greatness is supposed to be existence. A perfect being would not be perfect if it did not exist. Consequently, from the definition of God it is supposed to follow that he or she necessarily exists just as it follows from the definition of a triangle that the sum of its interior angles will be 180 degrees.

This argument, which has been used by several philosophers, including René Descartes (1596–1650) in the fifth of his *Meditations*, has convinced very few people of God's existence, but it is not easy to see precisely what is wrong with it.

CRITICISMS OF THE ONTOLOGICAL ARGUMENT

ABSURD CONSEQUENCES

One common criticism of the Ontological Argument is that it would seem to allow us to define all kinds of things into existence. For instance, we can quite easily imagine a perfect island, with a perfect beach, perfect wildlife, and so on, but it obviously does not follow from this that this perfect island actually exists somewhere. So, because the Ontological Argument seems to justify such a ridiculous conclusion, it can easily be seen to be a bad argument. Either the argument's structure must be unsound, or else at least one of its initial assumptions must be false; otherwise it could not possibly give rise to such obviously absurd consequences.

A defender of the Ontological Argument might well reply to this objection that, although it is clearly absurd to think that we can define the perfect island into existence, it is not absurd to think that from the definition of God it follows that God necessarily exists. This is because perfect islands, or for that matter perfect cars, perfect days, or whatever, are only perfect examples of particular kinds of things. But God is a special case: God is not just a perfect example of a kind, but the most perfect of all things.

However, even if this implausible argument is accepted, there is a further criticism of the Ontological Argument which any defender of it will have to meet. This further criticism was originally made by Immanuel Kant (1724–1804).

EXISTENCE IS NOT A PROPERTY

A bachelor can be defined as an unmarried man. Being unmarried is the *essential* defining property of a bachelor. Now, if I were to say 'bachelors exist', I would not be giving a further property of bachelors. Existence is not the same sort of thing as the property of being unmarried: for anyone to be unmarried they must first exist, though the concept of a bachelor remains the same whether or not any bachelors do happen to exist.

If we apply the same thinking to the Ontological Argument, we see that the mistake it makes is to treat the existence of God as if it were simply another property, like omniscience, or omnipotence. But God could not be omniscient or omnipotent without existing, so by giving a definition of God at all we are already assuming that he or she exists. Listing existence as a further essential property of a perfect being is making the mistake of treating existence as a property rather than as the precondition of anything having any properties at all.

But what about fictional beings, such as unicorns? Surely we can talk about the properties of a unicorn, such as having one horn and four legs, without unicorns actually having to exist. The answer is that what a sentence like 'Unicorns have one horn' really means is 'If unicorns were to exist, they would have one horn'. In other words, 'Unicorns have one horn' is really a hypothetical statement. So the non-existence of unicorns is not a problem for the view that existence is not a property.

EVIL

Even if the Ontological Argument is accepted, there is still much evidence that at least one aspect of its conclusion is false. The presence of evil in the world seems to oppose the idea that God is all-good. I deal with possible answers to this point in the section on the Problem of Evil.

KNOWLEDGE, PROOF, AND THE EXISTENCE OF GOD

The arguments for God's existence which we have considered so far have all at times been presented as *proofs*. They are supposed to yield knowledge of God's existence.

Knowledge in this context can be defined as a kind of true, justified belief. If we were to have knowledge that God exists it would have to be true that God actually does exist. But our belief that God exists would also have to be justified: it would have to be based on the right sort of evidence. It is possible to have beliefs that are true but unjustified: for example, I may believe that it is Tuesday because I have looked at what is written on what I believe is today's newspaper. But in fact I was looking at an old paper which just happened to have come out on a Tuesday. Although I believe that it is Tuesday (which it is), I did not acquire my belief in a reliable way, since I could just as easily have picked up an old newspaper which would have convinced me it was Thursday. So I did not really have knowledge, though I may mistakenly have thought that I did.

All the arguments for the existence of God that we have examined so far have been open to a number of objections. Whether these objections are sound or not is for you to decide. Certainly the objections should raise doubts about whether or not these arguments can be considered *proofs* of God's existence. But could we perhaps have knowledge – this type of true, justified belief – that God does *not* exist? In other words, are there any arguments which could conclusively disprove the existence of the God described by the Theists?

There is indeed at least one very strong argument against the existence of a benevolent God, one which I have already mentioned as a criticism of the Design, First Cause, and Ontological Arguments. This is the so-called Problem of Evil.

THE PROBLEM OF EVIL

There is evil in the world: this cannot seriously be denied. Think only of the Holocaust, of Pol Pot's massacres in Cambodia, or of the widespread practice of torture. These are all examples of moral evil or cruelty: human beings inflicting suffering on other human beings, for whatever reason. Cruelty is also often inflicted upon animals. There is also a different kind of evil, known as natural or metaphysical evil: earthquakes, disease, and famine are examples of this sort of evil.

Natural evil has natural causes, though it may be worsened by human incompetence or lack of care. 'Evil' may not be the most appropriate word to describe such natural phenomena, which give rise to human suffering, because the word is usually used to refer to deliberate cruelty. However, whether we label them 'natural evil' or choose another name for them, the existence of such things as disease and natural disaster certainly has to be accounted for if we are to maintain a belief in a benevolent God. Why would a god who cares about human beings create childhood leukemia or malaria? Why would such a god allow earthquakes and tsunamis to take place?

In view of the existence of so much evil, how can anyone seriously believe in the existence of an all-good God? An all-knowing God would know that evil exists; an all-powerful God would be able to prevent it occurring; and an all-good God would not want it to exist. But evil continues to occur. This is the Problem of Evil: the problem of explaining how the alleged attributes of God can be compatible with this undeniable fact of evil. This is the most serious challenge to belief in the Theists' God. The Problem of Evil has led many people to reject belief in God altogether, or at least to revise their opinion about God's supposed benevolence, omnipotence, or omniscience.

Theists have suggested a number of solutions to the Problem of Evil, three of which we will consider here. Such attempted explanations of how evil is compatible with the existence of God are usually known as theodicies.

ATTEMPTED SOLUTIONS TO THE PROBLEM OF EVIL

SAINTLINESS

Some people have argued that, though the presence of evil in the world is clearly not a good thing in itself, it is justified because it can lead to greater moral goodness. Without poverty and disease, for instance, Mother Teresa's great moral goodness in helping the needy would not have been possible. Without war, torture, and cruelty, no saints or heroes could exist. Evil allows the supposedly greater good of this kind of triumph over human suffering. However, such a solution is open to at least two objections. First, the degree and extent of suffering are far greater than would be necessary to allow saints and heroes to perform their acts of great moral goodness. It is extremely difficult to justify the horrific deaths of millions of people in Nazi concentration camps using this argument. Besides, much of this suffering goes unnoticed and unrecorded, and so cannot be explained in this way: in some cases the suffering individual is the only person capable of moral improvement in such a situation, and this improvement would be highly unlikely to occur in cases of extreme pain.

Second, it is not obvious that a world in which great evil exists would be preferable to one in which there was less evil and as a result fewer saints and heroes. Indeed, there is something offensive, for example, about trying to justify the agony of a young child dying of an incurable disease by arguing that this allows those witnessing this to become morally better people. Would an all-good God really use such methods to aid our moral development?

ARTISTIC ANALOGY

Some people have claimed that there is an analogy between the world and a work of art. Overall harmony in a piece of music usually involves discords which are subsequently resolved; a painting typically has large areas of darker as well as of lighter pigment. In a similar way, so the argument goes, evil contributes to the overall harmony or beauty of the world. This view is also open to at least two objections.

First, it is just difficult to believe. For instance, it is hard to understand how somebody dying in agony on a barbed-wire fence in no-man's-land in the Battle of the Somme could be said to have been contributing to the overall harmony of the world. If the analogy with a work of art is really the explanation of why God permits so much evil, then this is almost an admission that evil cannot satisfactorily be explained since it puts the understanding of evil beyond a merely human comprehension. It is only from God's viewpoint that the harmony could be observed and appreciated. If this is what it means when Theists say that God is all-good, then it is a very different use of the word 'good' from our usual one.

Second, a God who allows such suffering for merely aesthetic purposes – in order to appreciate it in the way one appreciates a work of art – sounds more like a sadist than the all-good deity described by Theists. If this is the role suffering plays, then it makes God uncomfortably close to the psychopath who throws a bomb into a crowd in order to admire the beautiful patterns created by the explosion and the blood. For many people this analogy between a work of art and the world would be more successful as an argument *against* God's benevolence than for it.

THE FREE WILL DEFENCE

By far the most important attempt at a solution to the Problem of Evil is the Free Will Defence. This is the claim that God has given human beings free will: the ability to choose for ourselves what to do. If we did not have free will we would be like robots, or automata, with no choices of our own. Those who accept the Free Will Defence argue that it is a necessary consequence of having free will that we should have the possibility of doing evil; otherwise it would not genuinely be free will. They tell us that a world in which human beings have free will which sometimes leads to evil is preferable to one in which human action is predetermined, one in which we would be like robots, programmed only to perform good actions. Indeed, if we were pre-programmed in this way, we could not even call our actions morally good since moral goodness depends on having a choice about what we do. Again, there are a number of objections to this proposed solution.

CRITICISMS OF THE FREE WILL DEFENCE

IT MAKES TWO BASIC ASSUMPTIONS

The main assumption that the Free Will Defence makes is that a world with free will and the possibility of evil is preferable to a world of robot-like people who never perform evil actions. But is this obviously so? Suffering can be so terrible that no doubt many people, given the choice, would prefer everyone to have been pre-programmed only to do good, rather than have to undergo such pain. These pre-programmed beings could even have been designed so that they believed they had free will even though they didn't: they could have had the illusion of free will with all the benefits that follow from thinking that they are free, but with none of the drawbacks.

This hints at a second assumption that the Free Will Defence makes, namely that we do actually have free will and not just an illusion of it. Some psychologists believe that we can explain every decision or choice that an individual makes by referring to some earlier conditioning that the individual has undergone, so that, although the individual might feel free, his or her action is in fact entirely determined by what has happened in the past, and by genetically transmitted predispositions. We cannot know for certain that this isn't actually the case.

However, it should be pointed out in the Free Will Defence's favour that most philosophers believe that human beings do have free will in some sense, and that free will is generally considered essential to being human.

FREE WILL BUT NO EVIL

If God is omnipotent, then presumably it is within his or her powers to have created a world in which there was both free will and yet no evil. In fact such a world is not particularly difficult to imagine. Although having free will always gives us the possibility of performing evil, there is no reason why this should ever become an actuality. It is logically possible that everyone could have had free will but decided always to shun the evil course of behaviour.

Those who accept the Free Will Defence would probably reply to this that such a state of affairs would not be genuine free will. This is open to debate.

GOD COULD INTERVENE

Theists typically believe that God can and does intervene in the world, primarily by performing miracles. If God intervenes some-times, why does he or she choose to perform what can seem to a non-believer relatively minor 'tricks' such as producing stigmata (marks on people's hands, like the nail holes in Christ's hands) or changing water into wine? Why didn't God intervene to prevent the Holocaust or the whole Second World War or the AIDS epidemic?

Again, Theists might reply that if God ever intervened then we would not have genuine free will. But this would be to abandon an aspect of most Theists' belief in God, namely that divine intervention sometimes occurs.

DOESN'T EXPLAIN NATURAL EVIL

A major criticism of the Free Will Defence is that it can at best only justify the existence of moral evil, evil brought about directly by human beings. There is no conceivable connection between having free will and the existence of such natural evil as earthquakes, disease, volcanic eruptions, and so on, unless one accepts some kind of doctrine of the Fall whereby Adam and Eve's betrayal of God's trust is supposed to have brought all the different sorts of evil on the world. The doctrine of the Fall makes human beings responsible for every form of evil in the world. However, such a doctrine would only be acceptable to someone who already believed in the existence of the Judaeo-Christian God.

There are other more plausible explanations of natural evil, one of which is that the regularity in the laws of nature has a great overall benefit which outweighs the occasional disasters that it gives rise to.

BENEFICIAL LAWS OF NATURE

Without regularity in nature our world would be mere chaos, and we would have no way of predicting the results of any of our actions. If, for instance, footballs only sometimes left our feet when we kicked them, sometimes simply sticking to them, then we would have great difficulty predicting what was going to happen on any particular occasion when we went to kick a ball. Lack of regularity in other aspects of the world might make life itself impossible. Science, as well as everyday life, relies upon there being a great deal of regularity in nature, similar causes tending to produce similar effects.

Some Theists argue that because this regularity is usually beneficial to us, natural evil is justified since it is just an unfortunate side-effect of the laws of nature continuing to operate in a regular way. The overall beneficial effects of this regularity are supposed to outweigh the detrimental ones. But this argument is vulnerable in at least two ways.

First, it does not explain why an omnipotent God couldn't have created laws of nature which would never actually lead to any natural evil. A possible response to this is that even God is bound by the laws of nature; but this suggests that God is not really omnipotent.

Second, it still fails to explain why God does not intervene to perform miracles more often. If he or she never intervenes, then, as we have seen, a major aspect of most Theists' belief in God is taken away.

THE ARGUMENT FROM MIRACLES

In discussing the Problem of Evil and attempted solutions to it, I mentioned that Theists usually believe that God has performed occasional miracles: in the Christian tradition these include the Resurrection, the feeding of the five thousand, bringing Lazarus back from the dead, and so on. These were all miracles which Christ allegedly performed, but it is often claimed by Christianity and other religions that miracles occur now. Here we shall consider whether the claim that miracles have occurred could ever provide sufficient evidence for believing in the existence of God.

A miracle can be defined as some kind of divine intervention in the normal course of events which involves breaking an established law of nature. A law of nature is a generalization about the way certain things behave: for example, weights fall to the ground when dropped, no one rises from the dead, and so on. Such laws of nature are based on a large number of observations.

Miracles should at the outset be distinguished from merely extraordinary occurrences. Someone may try to commit suicide by jumping off a high bridge. By a freak combination of factors, such as wind conditions, their clothes acting as a parachute, and so on, they may – as has happened – survive the fall. Whilst this is extremely unusual, and might even be described by the newspapers as 'a miracle', it is not a miracle in the sense I am using the term here. We could give a satisfactory scientific explanation of how this individual came to survive: it was only an extraordinary event, not a miraculous one, since no law of nature was broken, and, as far as we can tell, no divine intervention was involved. If, however, the person had jumped from the bridge and had mysteriously bounced off the river back up on to the bridge, then that would indeed have been a miracle.

Most religions claim that God has performed miracles, and that the reports of these miracles should be treated as confirmation that God exists. However, there are strong arguments against basing a belief in God on such reported miracles.

HUME ON MIRACLES

David Hume, in Section X of his *Enquiry Concerning Human Understanding*, argued that a rational person should never believe a report that a miracle had actually taken place unless it would be a greater miracle that the person reporting the miracle was mistaken. This, he argued, is highly unlikely ever to be so. We should, as a policy, always believe whatever would be the lesser miracle. In this statement Hume is deliberately playing on the meaning of 'miracle'. As we have already seen, a miracle in the strict sense is a transgression of a law of nature presumed to have been caused by God. However, when Hume declares that we should believe whatever is the lesser miracle, he is using the word 'miracle' in the everyday sense, which can include something which is merely out of the ordinary.

Although he allowed that miracles might in principle occur, Hume thought that there had never been a reliable enough report of a miracle on which to base a belief in God. He used several powerful arguments to support this view.

MIRACLES ALWAYS IMPROBABLE

Hume first of all analysed the evidence that we have that any particular law of nature holds. For something to be accepted as a law of nature – for instance, that no one ever rises from the dead – there must be the maximum possible amount of evidence confirming it.

A wise person will always base what they believe on the available evidence. And in the case of any report of a miracle there will always be more evidence to suggest that it didn't occur than that it did. This is just a consequence of miracles involving the breaking of well-established laws of nature. So, using this argument, a wise person should always be extremely reluctant to believe a report that a miracle has occurred. It is always logically possible that someone could rise from the dead, but there is a great amount of evidence supporting the view that this has never happened. So although we cannot absolutely rule out the possibility that the Resurrection occurred, according to Hume, we should be extremely reluctant to believe that it did.

Hume gave several further arguments to make this conclusion more convincing.

PSYCHOLOGICAL FACTORS

Psychological factors can lead people to be self-deceived or even actually fraudulent about the occurrence of miracles. For instance, it is a well-observed fact that amazement and wonder are pleasant emotions. We have a strong tendency to believe highly improbable things – such as that UFO sightings prove the existence of intelligent life on Mars, that ghost stories demonstrate the possibility of life after death, and the like – because of the pleasure that we experience in entertaining such fantastic beliefs. Similarly we are prone to believe reports of miracles, since most of us would, secretly or otherwise, like such reports to be true.

Also it is extremely appealing to think that you have been chosen to witness a miracle, that you are some kind of prophet. Many people would enjoy the approval that others give to those who claim to have witnessed miracles. This can lead them to interpret merely extraordinary events as miracles revealing God's presence. It may even lead them to concoct stories about miraculous events.

RELIGIONS CANCEL OUT

Miracles have been claimed by all the major religions. There is a similar amount of evidence of a similar kind that miracles claimed by each of these religions have really happened. Consequently the Argument from Miracles, if it were reliable, would prove the existence of the different gods of each religion. But clearly these different gods cannot all exist: it can't be true that there is only one Christian God *and* the many Hindu ones. So the miracles claimed by the different religions cancel each other out as proofs of the existence of a particular God or gods.

The combination of these factors should always make rational people reluctant to believe reports that a miracle has happened. A natural explanation, even if improbable in itself, is always more likely to be appropriate than a miraculous one. Certainly a report of a miracle could never amount to a proof of God's existence.

These arguments are not restricted to other people's reports of miracles. If we ourselves are in the unusual position of thinking that we have witnessed a miracle, most of them still apply. We have all experienced dreams, cases of misremembering things, or of thinking we have seen things which weren't really there. In any case in which we believe we have witnessed a miracle, it is far more likely that our senses have deceived us than that a miracle has actually occurred. Or else we may only have witnessed something extraordinary and, due to the psychological factors mentioned above, thought it was a miracle.

Of course anyone who thinks they have witnessed a miracle would, rightly, take this experience very seriously. But, because it is so easy to be mistaken about these things, such an experience should never count as a conclusive proof of God's existence.

THE GAMBLER'S ARGUMENT: PASCAL'S WAGER

The arguments for and against the existence of God that we have examined so far have all been aimed at proving that God does or doesn't exist. They have all purported to give us knowledge of his or her existence or non-existence. The Gambler's Argument, which is derived from the writings of the philosopher and mathematician Blaise Pascal (1623–62), and is usually known as 'Pascal's Wager', is very different from these. Its aim is not to provide proof, but rather to show that a sensible gambler would be well advised to 'bet' that God exists.

It begins from the position of an agnostic, that is, someone who believes that there is not enough evidence to decide whether or not God exists. An atheist, in contrast, typically believes that there is conclusive evidence that God does not exist.

The Gambler's Argument proceeds as follows. Since we do not know whether or not God exists, we are in much the same position as a gambler before a race has been run or a card turned. We must then calculate the odds. But to the agnostic it may seem just as likely that God exists as that he or she doesn't. The agnostic's course of action is to sit on the fence, not making a decision either way. The Gambler's Argument, however, says that the most rational thing to do is to aim to have a chance of winning as great a prize as possible, whilst keeping our chance of losing as small as possible: in other words, we should maximize our possible winnings, and minimize our possible losses. According to the Gambler's Argument, the best way to do this is to believe in God.

There are four possible outcomes. If we bet on the existence of God and win (i.e. if God does exist), then we gain eternal life – a great prize. What we lose if we bet on this option and it turns out that God doesn't exist is not great when compared with the possibility of eternal life: we may miss out on certain worldly pleasures, waste many hours praying, and live our lives under an illusion. However, if we choose to bet on the option that God doesn't exist, and we win (i.e. if God doesn't exist), then we live a life without illusion (at least in this respect), and feel free to indulge in the pleasures of this life without fear of divine punishment. But if we bet on this option and lose (i.e. if God does exist), then we at least miss the chance of eternal life, and may even run the risk of eternal damnation.

Pascal argued that, as gamblers faced with these options, the most rational course of action for us is to believe that God does exist. This way, if we are correct, we stand to win eternal life. If we gamble that God exists and are wrong we do not stand to lose so much as if we choose to believe that God doesn't exist and are wrong. So, if we want to maximize our possible gains and minimize our possible losses, then we ought to believe in God's existence.

CRITICISMS OF THE GAMBLER'S ARGUMENT

CAN'T DECIDE TO BELIEVE

Even if the Gambler's Argument is accepted, we are still left with the problem that it is not possible for us to believe in whatever we want. We can't simply decide to believe something. I can't decide tomorrow to believe that pigs can fly, that London is the capital of Egypt, or that an all-powerful, all-knowing, and all-good God exists. I need to be convinced that these things are so before I can believe them. But the Gambler's Argument provides no evidence whatsoever to convince me that God does exist: it merely tells me that as a gambler I would be well advised to bring myself to believe this to be so. But here I am faced with the problem that, in order to believe anything, I must believe that it is true.

Pascal had a solution to this problem of how to make ourselves believe that God exists if this goes against our feelings on the matter. He suggested that the way to do this was to act as if we already believed that God existed: go to church, say the words of the appropriate prayers, and so on. He argued that if we gave the out-ward signs of a belief in God, then very quickly we would develop the actual beliefs. In other words, there are indirect ways in which we can deliberately generate beliefs.

INAPPROPRIATE ARGUMENT

To gamble that God does exist because we thereby gain the chance of everlasting life, and then to trick ourselves into an actual belief in God because of the prize we win if we are correct, seems an inappropriate attitude to take to the question of God's existence. The philosopher and psychologist William James (1842–1910) went so far as to say that if he were in God's position he would take great delight in preventing people who believed in him on the basis of this procedure from going to heaven. The whole procedure seems insincere, and is entirely motivated by self-interest.

NON-REALISM ABOUT GOD

Non-realism about God provides a controversial alternative to traditional Theism. Non-realists argue that it is a mistake to think of God as something existing independently of human beings. The true meaning of religious language is not to describe some sort of objectively existing being; rather it is a way of representing to ourselves the ideal unity of all our moral and spiritual values, and the claims these values have upon us. In other words, when a non-realist of this kind claims to believe in God this doesn't mean that he or she believes in God as an entity which actually exists in a separate realm, the sort of God described by traditional Theists. Instead they mean that they commit themselves to a particular set of moral and spiritual values, and that the language of religion provides an especially powerful way of representing these values. As Don Cupitt (1934–), one of the best-known non-realists, has put it, 'To speak of God is to speak about the moral and spiritual goals we ought to be aiming at, and about what we ought to become.'

According to non-realists, those who believe that God exists as something out there to be discovered like another planet or the yeti are in the grip of mythological thinking. The true meaning of religious language, they claim, is to represent to ourselves the highest human ideals. This explains how different religions came into existence: they have grown up as an embodiment of different cultural values, but in a sense they are all part of the same sort of activity.

CRITICISMS OF NON-REALISM ABOUT GOD

DISGUISED ATHEISM

The main criticism of non-realism about God is that it is a thinly disguised kind of atheism. To say that God is simply the sum of human values is tantamount to saying that God as traditionally conceived does not exist; religious language just provides a useful way of talking about values in a godless world. This can appear hypocritical, since non-realists reject the idea that God has an objective existence and yet at the same time want to cling to religious language and ritual. It seems more honest to follow through the consequence of believing that God doesn't really exist and become an atheist.

IMPLICATIONS FOR RELIGIOUS DOCTRINE

A second criticism of the non-realist approach to the question of God's existence is that it has very serious implications for religious doctrine. For instance, most Theists believe in the existence of heaven; but if God doesn't really exist, then presumably nor does heaven (nor, for that matter, hell). Similarly, if God does not exist in a realist sense, it is difficult to see how a plausible account of miracles could be given. Yet belief in the possibility of miracles is a central one for many Theists. Adopting a non-realist stance to the question of God's existence would involve radical revision of many basic religious beliefs. This in itself need not undermine the non-realist approach: if someone is prepared to accept such radical revisions then they can consistently do so. The point is that the non-realist view involves a substantial overhaul of basic religious doctrine, an overhaul that many people would not be prepared to make.

FAITH

All the arguments for God's existence that we have examined have been subject to criticisms. These criticisms are not necessarily conclusive. You may be able to find counter-criticisms. But if you can't find suitable counter-criticisms, does this mean that you should reject belief in God altogether? Atheists would say that you should. Agnostics would return a verdict of 'not proven'. Religious believers, however, might argue that the philosophical approach, weighing up different arguments, is inappropriate. Belief in God, they might say, is not a matter for abstract intellectual speculation, but rather for personal commitment. It is a matter of faith, not of the clever employment of reason.

Faith involves trust. If I'm climbing a mountain and I put my faith in the strength of my rope, then I trust that it will hold me if I should lose my footing and fall, though I can't be absolutely certain that it will hold me until I put it to the test. For some people, faith in God is like faith in the strength of the rope: there is no established proof that God exists and cares for every individual, but the believer trusts that God does indeed exist and lives his or her life accordingly.

An attitude of religious faith is attractive to many people. It makes the kind of arguments we have been considering irrelevant. Yet at its most extreme, religious faith can make people completely blind to the evidence against their views: it can become more like stubbornness than a rational attitude.

What are the dangers of adopting such an attitude of faith towards God's existence if you have an inclination to do so?

THE DANGERS OF FAITH

Faith, as I have described it, is based on insufficient evidence. If there were sufficient evidence to declare that God exists, then there would be less need for faith: we would then have knowledge that God exists. Because there is insufficient evidence to be certain of God's existence, there is always the possibility that the faithful are mistaken in their faith. And, as with the belief that miracles have occurred, there are a number of psychological factors which can lead people to put their faith in God.

For instance, the security that comes from believing that an all-powerful being is looking after us is undeniably attractive. Belief in life after death is a good antidote to a fear of death. These factors can be incentives for some to commit themselves to a faith in God. Of course, this doesn't necessarily make their faith misplaced, it simply shows that the causes of their faith may be a combination of insecurity and wishful thinking.

Also, as Hume argued, human beings get a great deal of pleasure from the feelings of wonder and amazement that come from believing in paranormal occurrences. In the case of putting one's faith in God, it is important to distinguish a genuine faith from the pleasure derived from entertaining the belief that God exists.

These psychological factors should make us wary about committing ourselves to faith in God: it is so easy to be mistaken about one's motivation in this area. In the end, each believer must judge whether or not his or her faith is appropriate and genuine.

DEATH

Most people who believe in the existence of some kind of God also believe in an afterlife. Some atheists also believe in an afterlife, but typically they do not. If you believe in an afterlife you have less reason to fear your own death than if you don't, provided, of course, that the afterlife is likely to be a pleasant one and not eternal damnation. Either way, for those who believe in an afterlife death is not the end of everything.

IS FEAR OF DEATH IRRATIONAL?

Fear of death is widespread, and belief in God and an afterlife can be a consolation for those whose lives are unpleasant or painful. Yet belief in an afterlife might just be wishful thinking. Some philosophers have argued that even if death is completely final we have nothing to fear. Others have made the case that a finite existence is preferable to immortality.

Epicurus (341–271 BC) tried to show that we have no reason to fear death. Fear of death arises from mistakenly imagining that we will be there after our deaths to mourn our own loss. But when we are alive, death is absent; and when we are dead, we no longer exist to be harmed. So either we are alive, and death isn't harming us; or we are dead, and then there is nothing to be harmed. Furthermore, he argued, we don't usually worry about the eternity of our non-existence before birth, so we shouldn't worry in the least about the eternity of our non-existence after death. His conclusion was that fear of death is irrational. This, of course, still allows that it may be perfectly rational to fear the process of dying and the pain that typically accompanies it.

CRITICISM OF EPICURUS

ASSUMES ANY AFTERLIFE WON'T BE BAD

Epicurus assumes that any afterlife won't be bad. Both his arguments are arguments about the fear of our own non-existence. They do not take account of fear of what might happen to us following death. If there is an afterlife, there might be aspects of that afterlife that it would be completely rational to fear, the possibility of spending eternity being boiled in sulphur and being prodded by little devils with tridents, for instance. Another possibility that has been seriously suggested is that immortality would end up being tedious, something that we might have very good reason to fear.

WOULD IMMORTALITY BE TEDIOUS?

Many human activities gain their meaning from the fact that they are unrepeatable. We make choices, decisions that shape the people we become. Our joy in the immediate experience of the pattern of light and shade in a forest partly comes from the fact that it is a transient effect that we may never see again. Our mortality makes us value the present because we may not have a future. The pattern of our choices and the things that happen to us give us our personal history. Yet if we are going to live for ever after death, this source of meaning won't be there for us. There will always be time to do everything. Bernard Williams (1929–2003) argued that such immortality would be tedious and ultimately meaningless. It is the fact of death and its finality that gives our lives much of the meaning that they have.

CRITICISM OF THE TEDIUM OF IMMORTALITY

ASSUMES THE AFTERLIFE IS LIKE THE PRESENT LIFE

The lack of meaning and boredom that would go with having time to do anything and everything are a projection of what we experience in this world to the next. Yet, presumably a benevolent God wouldn't want us to be bored in the afterlife, so we can be confident if such a being exists that the afterlife will be very different from life on Earth in ways that we cannot imagine.

If this is so, however, it raises the question of whether any such afterlife is a life that *we* carry on living, since what we are is so shaped by our finite existence in time and the knowledge that we will die. In what sense is such a life for *me* since what I am has been so bound up with the decisions that I have made about how I spend my limited time? If the response to this question is that this is something that God will take care of, then this is a recourse to faith again, with the possibility that this faith might be misplaced.

CONCLUSION

In this chapter we have considered most of the traditional arguments for and against the existence of God. We have seen that there are serious criticisms which Theists need to meet if they are to maintain a belief in an omnipotent, omniscient, supremely benevolent God. One way of meeting many of these criticisms would be to revise the qualities usually attributed to God: perhaps God is not entirely benevolent, or perhaps there are limits to his or her power, or knowledge. To do so would be to reject the traditional account of God. But for many people this would be a more acceptable solution than rejecting belief in God altogether.

FURTHER READING

I thoroughly recommend J. L. Mackie's *The Miracle of Theism* (Oxford: Clarendon Press, 1982). It is clear, intelligent, and stimulating. It deals in greater detail with most of the issues covered in this chapter. Brian Davies's *An Introduction to the Philosophy of Religion* (2nd edition, Oxford: Oxford University Press, 1993) is a comprehensive introduction to this area written by a Dominican Friar. Beverley and Brian Clack's *The Philosophy of Religion: A Critical Introduction* (Cambridge: Polity, 1998) is another useful guide to this area of thought. Julian Baggini's *Atheism: A Very Short Introduction* (Oxford: Oxford University Press, 2003) is a positive account of life without God. Robin Le Poidevin's *Arguing for Atheism* (London: Routledge, 1996) is an interesting and wide-ranging book which also serves as an introduction to some important areas of metaphysics such as the nature of time.

David Hume's posthumous *Dialogues Concerning Natural Religion*, first published in 1779, contains a brilliant and sustained attack on the Design Argument for God's existence. The eighteenth-century prose can be quite difficult to understand in places, but the main arguments are easy to follow and are illustrated with witty and memorable examples. The best edition is David Hume's *Dialogues and Natural History of Religion* (Oxford: Oxford University Press World's Classics, 1993). I give a brief introduction to the main themes of Hume's book in *Philosophy: The Classics* (2nd edition, London: Routledge, 2001).

Don Cupitt outlines his non-realist alternative to Theism in the final chapter of his book *The Sea of Faith* (London: BBC Books, 1984) and in his *Taking Leave of God* (London: SCM Press, 2001).

Recent popular books defending atheism include Richard Dawkins's polemical *The God Delusion* (London: Bantam Press, 2006), and Sam Harris's *Letter to a Christian Nation* (New York: Knopf, 2006). On the other side of the debate, Alister McGrath's *Why God Won't Go Away: Engaging with the New Atheism* (London: SPCK Publishing, 2011) addresses atheists' objections to religion from a Christian perspective.

2

RIGHT AND WRONG

What makes an action right or wrong? What do we mean when we say that someone ought or ought not to do something? How should we live? How should we treat other people? These are fundamental questions which philosophers have argued about for thousands of years. If we cannot say why such things as torture, murder, cruelty, slavery, rape, and theft are wrong, what justification can we have for trying to prevent them? Is morality simply a matter of prejudice or can we give good reasons for our moral beliefs? The area of philosophy which deals with such questions is usually known either as ethics or as moral philosophy – I shall use the terms interchangeably here.

I am sceptical of philosophy's ability to change people's fundamental prejudices about what is right or wrong. As Friedrich Nietzsche (1844–1900) pointed out in *Beyond Good and Evil*, most moral philosophers end up justifying 'a desire of the heart that has been filtered and made abstract'. In other words, these philosophers give complicated analyses which appear to involve impersonal logical reasoning but which always end up by demonstrating that their pre-existing prejudices were correct. Nevertheless moral philosophy can provide insights when dealing with real moral issues: it can clarify the implications of certain very general beliefs about morality, and show how these beliefs can consistently be put into practice. Here I will examine three types of moral theory: duty-based, consequentialist, and virtue-based. These are very general competing frameworks for understanding moral issues. First I will outline the main features of these three sorts of theory and show how they might be applied to a real-life case. I will then go on to the more abstract philosophical questions about the meaning of moral language, known as meta-ethics.

DUTY-BASED THEORIES

Duty-based ethical theories stress that each of us has certain duties – actions that we ought or ought not to perform – and that acting morally amounts to doing our duty, whatever consequences might follow from this. It is this idea, that some actions are absolutely right or wrong regardless of the results which follow from them, which distinguishes duty-based (also known as deontological) ethical theories from consequentialist ethical theories. Here we will examine two duty-based theories: Christian ethics and Kantian ethics.

CHRISTIAN ETHICS

Judaeo-Christian moral teaching has dominated Western understanding of morality: our whole conception of what morality is has been shaped by religious doctrine, and even atheistic ethical theories are heavily indebted to it. The Ten Commandments list various duties and forbidden activities. These duties apply regardless of the consequences of carrying them out: they are absolute duties. Someone who believes that the Bible is the word of God will have no doubt about the meaning of 'right' and 'wrong': 'right' means what God wills, and 'wrong' means anything which is against God's will. For such a believer morality is a matter of following absolute commands given by the external authority, God. So, for instance, killing is always morally wrong because it is explicitly listed as a sin in the Ten Commandments. This is so even when killing a particular individual – Hitler for instance – might save other people's lives. This is a simplification: in fact theologians do argue about exceptional circumstances when killing might be morally permissible, as for instance in a just war.

In practice, Christian morality is far more complicated than just obeying the Ten Commandments: it involves the application of

Christ's teaching, and in particular of the New Testament Commandment 'Love thy neighbour'. The essence of this morality, however, is a system of dos and don'ts. The same is true of most other moralities based on a religion.

Many people have thought that if God doesn't exist there can be no such thing as morality: as the Russian novelist Dostoevsky put it, 'If God doesn't exist, then anything is permitted'. Nevertheless, there are at least three major objections to any ethical theory based solely upon God's will.

CRITICISMS OF CHRISTIAN ETHICS

WHAT IS GOD'S WILL?

One immediate difficulty with Christian ethics is finding out what God's will actually is. How can we know for sure what God wants us to do? Christians usually answer this question by saying, 'Look at the Bible'. But the Bible is open to numerous, and often conflicting, interpretations: think only of the differences between those who take the Book of Genesis literally, believing that the world was created in seven days, and those who think that this is a metaphor; or of the differences between those who think that killing in war is sometimes acceptable and those who believe that the Commandment 'Thou shalt not kill' is absolute and unconditional.

THE *EUTHYPHRO* DILEMMA

A dilemma arises when there are only two possible alternatives and neither is desirable. In this case the dilemma is one that was originally presented in Plato's *Euthyphro*. The dilemma for someone who believes that morality is derived from God's commands is as follows. Does God command or love what he or she commands or loves because it is morally good? Or does God's commanding or loving it make it morally good?

Consider the first option. If God commands or loves what he or she commands or loves because it is morally good then this makes morality in some sense independent of God. He or she is responding to pre-existing moral values that occur in the universe: discovering rather than creating them. On this view it would be possible to describe morality completely without any mention of God, though it might be thought that God provides us with more reliable information about morality than we would otherwise be able to glean from the world with our limited intellects. Nevertheless, on this view, God is not the source of morality.

The second option is probably even less attractive to defenders of Christian ethics. If God creates right and wrong simply by his or her commands or approval then this seems to make morality somewhat arbitrary. In principle God could have declared murder to be morally praiseworthy and it would have been. A defender of morality as a system of God's commands might answer that God would never make murder morally praiseworthy because God is good and would not wish that upon us. But if by 'good' is meant 'morally good', this has the consequence that all that 'God is good' can mean is 'God approves of him- or herself'. This is hardly what believers mean when they say 'God is good'.

IT ASSUMES GOD'S EXISTENCE

However, a far more serious objection to such a view of ethics is that it presupposes that God actually exists and is benevolent. If God weren't benevolent, why would acts in accordance with his or her will be considered morally good? As we have seen in Chapter 1, neither God's existence nor benevolence can be taken for granted.

Not all duty based moral theories rely on God's existence. The most important duty-based moral theory, that of Immanuel Kant (1724–1804), although strongly influenced by the Protestant Christian tradition, and despite the fact that Kant himself was a devout Christian, describes morality in a way which, in its broadest outlines, many atheists have found appealing.

KANTIAN ETHICS

MOTIVES

Immanuel Kant was interested in the question 'What is a moral action?' The answer he gave has been of tremendous importance in philosophy. Here I will outline its main features.

For Kant it was clear that a moral action was one performed out of a sense of duty, rather than simply out of inclination or feeling or the possibility of some kind of gain for the person performing it. So, for example, if I give money to charity because I have deep feelings of compassion for the needy, I am, in Kant's view, not necessarily acting morally: if I act purely from my feelings of compassion rather than from a sense of duty, then my action is not a *moral* one. Or if I give money to charity because I think it will increase my popularity with my friends, then, again, I am not acting *morally*, but for gain in social status.

So for Kant the motive of an action was far more important than the action itself and its consequences. He thought that in order to know whether or not someone was acting morally you had to know what their intention was. It was not enough just to know whether or not the Good Samaritan helped the man in need. The Samaritan might have been acting out of self-interest, expecting a reward for his troubles. Or else he might have done it only because he felt a twinge of compassion: this would have been acting from an emotional motive rather than from a sense of duty.

Most other moral philosophers would agree with Kant that self-interest is not an appropriate motive for a moral action. But many would disagree with his claim that whether or not someone feels such an emotion as compassion is irrelevant to our moral assessment of their actions. For Kant, however, the only acceptable motive for moral action was a sense of duty.

One reason why Kant concentrated so much on the motives for actions rather than on their consequences was that he believed that all people could be moral. Since we can only reasonably be held morally responsible for things over which we have some control – or as he put it, since 'ought implies can' – and because the consequences of actions are often outside our control, these consequences cannot be crucial to morality. For instance, if, acting from my sense of duty, I attempt to save a drowning child, but accidentally drown the child, my action can still be considered a moral one since my motives were of the right kind: the consequences of my action would have been, in this case, tragic, but irrelevant to the moral worth of what I did.

Similarly, as we don't necessarily have complete control over our emotional reactions, these cannot be essential to morality either. If morality was to be available to all conscious human beings, then, Kant thought, it had to rely entirely upon the will, and in particular on our sense of duty.

MAXIMS

Kant described the intentions behind any act as the *maxim*. The maxim is the general principle underlying the action. For instance, the Good Samaritan could have been acting on the maxim 'Always help those in need if you expect you will be rewarded for your troubles'. Or he could have been acting on the maxim 'Always help those in need when you experience a feeling of compassion'. However, if the Good Samaritan's behaviour were moral, then he would probably have been acting on the maxim 'Always help those in need because it is your duty to do so'.

THE CATEGORICAL IMPERATIVE

Kant believed that as rational human beings we have certain duties. These duties are *categorical*: in other words they are absolute and unconditional – duties such as 'You ought always to tell the truth' or 'You ought never to kill anyone'. They apply whatever consequences might follow from obeying them. Kant thought morality was a system of Categorical Imperatives: commands to act in certain ways. This is one of the most distinctive aspects of his ethics. He contrasted categorical duties with *hypothetical* ones. A hypothetical duty is one such as 'If you want to be respected, then you ought to tell the truth' or 'If you want to avoid going to prison, then you ought not to murder anyone'. Hypothetical duties tell you what you ought or ought not to do if you want to achieve or avoid a certain goal. He thought there was only one basic Categorical Imperative: 'Act only on maxims which you can at the same time will to be universal laws'. 'Will' here means 'rationally want'. In other words, the message of the Categorical Imperative is only act on a maxim you would rationally want to apply to everybody. This principle is known as the principle of universalizability.

Although he gave a number of different versions of the Categorical Imperative, this is the most important of them and it has been immensely influential. We will examine it in more detail.

UNIVERSALIZABILITY

Kant thought that for an action to be moral, the underlying maxim had to be a universalizable one. It had to be a maxim that would hold for anyone else in similar circumstances. You should not make an exception of yourself, but should be impartial. So, for example, if you stole a book, acting on the maxim 'Always steal when you are too poor to buy what you want', for this to have been a moral act, this maxim would have had to apply to anyone else in your position.

Of course this doesn't mean that any maxim whatsoever which can be universalized is for that reason a moral one. It is obvious that many trivial maxims, such as 'Always poke your tongue out at people who are taller than you', could quite easily be universalized, even though they have little or nothing to do with morality. Some other universalizable maxims, such as the one about stealing, which I used in the previous paragraph, may still be considered immoral.

This notion of universalizability is a version of the so-called Golden Rule of Christianity, 'Do unto others as you would have them do unto you'. Someone acting on the maxim 'Be a parasite, always live at other people's expense' would not be acting morally since it would be impossible to universalize the maxim. It would invite the question, 'What if everyone did that?' And if everyone were parasites, then there would be no one left for parasites to live on. The maxim fails to pass Kant's test, and so cannot be a moral one.

On the other hand, we can quite easily universalize the maxim 'Never torture babies'. It is certainly possible and desirable for everyone to obey this order, although they may not. Those who disobey it by torturing babies are acting immorally. With maxims such as this one, Kant's notion of universalizability quite clearly gives an answer which corresponds to most people's unquestioned intuitions about right and wrong.

MEANS AND ENDS

Another of Kant's versions of the Categorical Imperative was 'Treat other people as ends in themselves, never as means to an end'. This is another way of saying that we should not *use* other people, but should always recognize their humanity: the fact that they are individuals with wills and desires of their own. If someone is pleasant to you simply because they know that you can give them a job, then they are treating you as a means to getting that job, and not as a person, as an end in yourself. Of course, if someone is pleasant to you because they happen to like you, that would not have anything to do with morality.

CRITICISMS OF KANTIAN ETHICS

IT IS EMPTY

Kant's ethical theory, and in particular his notion of the universalizability of moral judgements, is sometimes criticized for being empty. This means that his theory only gives a framework showing the structure of moral judgements without giving any help to those faced with making actual moral decisions. It gives little aid to people trying to decide what they ought to do.

This neglects the version of the Categorical Imperative which instructs us to treat people as ends and never solely as means. In this formulation Kant certainly does give some content to his moral theory. But even with the combination of the universalizability thesis and the means/ends formulation, Kant's theory does not yield satisfactory solutions to many moral questions.

For instance, Kant's theory cannot easily cope with conflicts of duty. If, for example, I have a duty always to tell the truth, and also a duty to protect my friends, Kant's theory would not show me what I ought to do when these two duties conflict. If a madman carrying an axe asked me where my friend was, my first inclination would be to tell him a lie. To tell the truth would be to shirk the duty I have to protect my friend. But on the other hand, according to Kant, to tell a lie, even in such an extreme situation, would be an immoral act: I have an absolute duty never to lie.

UNIVERSALIZABLE IMMORAL ACTS

A further related weakness that some people see in Kant's theory is that it seems to permit some obviously immoral acts. For instance, it appears that a maxim such as 'Kill anyone who gets in your way' could quite consistently be universalized. And yet such a maxim is clearly immoral.

But this sort of criticism fails as a criticism of Kant: it ignores the means/ends version of the Categorical Imperative, which it obviously contradicts. To kill someone who gets in your way is hardly treating them as an end in themselves: it is a failure to take their interests into account.

IMPLAUSIBLE ASPECTS

Though much of Kant's ethical theory is plausible – especially the idea of respecting other people's interests – it does have some implausible aspects. First, it seems to justify some absurd actions, such as telling a mad axeman where your friend is rather than putting him off the trail by telling him a lie.

Second, the role the theory gives to emotions such as compassion, sympathy, and pity seems inadequate. Kant dismisses such emotions as irrelevant to morality: the only appropriate motive for moral action is a sense of duty. Feeling compassion for someone in need, while it may be considered praiseworthy from some viewpoints, is not, for Kant, anything to do with morality. In contrast, many people think that there *are* distinctively moral emotions, such as compassion, sympathy, guilt, and remorse, and to separate these from morality, as Kant attempted to do, is to ignore a central aspect of moral behaviour.

Third, the theory takes no account of the consequences of actions. This means that well-intentioned idiots who unintentionally cause a number of deaths through incompetence might be morally blameless on Kant's theory. They would be judged primarily on their intentions. But in some cases consequences of actions do seem relevant to an assessment of their moral worth: think how you would feel about the well-intentioned babysitter who tried to dry your cat in a microwave oven. However, to be fair to Kant on this point, he does consider some kinds of incompetence culpable.

Those who find this last sort of criticism of deontological theories convincing will very likely see the appeal of the type of ethical theory known as consequentialism.

CONSEQUENTIALISM

The term 'consequentialist' is used to describe ethical theories which judge whether an action is right or wrong not on the intentions of the person performing the action, but rather on the consequences of that action. Whereas Kant would say that telling a lie was always morally wrong, whatever the possible benefits which might result, a consequentialist would judge the lie-telling on the results it had, or could be expected to have.

UTILITARIANISM

Utilitarianism is the best-known type of consequentialist ethical theory. Its most famous advocates were Jeremy Bentham (1748–1832) and John Stuart Mill (1806–73). Utilitarianism is based on the assumption that the ultimate aim of all human activity is (in some sense) happiness. Such a view is known as *hedonism*.

A utilitarian defines 'good' as 'whatever brings about the greatest total happiness'. This is sometimes known as the Greatest Happiness Principle or the Principle of Utility. For a utilitarian the right action in any circumstances can be calculated by examining the probable consequences of the various possible courses of action. Whichever is most likely to bring about the most happiness (or at least the greatest balance of happiness over unhappiness) is the right action in those circumstances.

Utilitarianism has to deal in *probable* consequences because it is usually extremely difficult, if not impossible, to predict the precise results of any particular action: for example, insulting people usually makes them feel unhappy, but the person you are insulting may turn out to be a masochist who takes great pleasure from being insulted.

One of the advantages of utilitarianism over some other approaches to ethics is that it can give a clear method for including animals within the realm of moral concern. Provided that it is accepted that animals are capable of pain and pleasure, then it is possible to include their welfare in the utilitarian calculation. And even if animals are not directly included in the calculation, the fact that their apparent suffering has an effect on the happiness of animal-lovers allows their welfare to be included in the assessment indirectly. For example, if I and others like me are deeply distressed by the knowledge that calves suffer in the production of veal, our unhappiness needs to be set against the possible pleasures experienced by consumers of veal when deciding the morality of veal production. Chapter 3 deals more thoroughly with questions about the moral status of non-human animals.

CRITICISMS OF UTILITARIANISM

DIFFICULTIES OF CALCULATION

Whilst utilitarianism may sound an attractive theory in principle, there are many difficulties which arise when you try to put it into practice.

It is extremely difficult to measure happiness and to compare the happiness of different people. Who is to decide whether or not the great pleasure experienced by a sadist outweighs the victim's suffering? Or how does the pleasure a football fan experiences watching his or her team score a brilliant goal compare with the tingles of delight experienced by an opera buff listening to a favourite aria? And how do these compare with the more physical sensations of pleasure such as those that come from sex and eating?

Bentham thought that in principle such comparisons could be made. For him, the source of happiness was irrelevant. Happiness was simply a blissful mental state: pleasure and the absence of pain. Although it occurred in different intensities, it was all of the same kind and so, however produced, should be given weight in utilitarian calculations. In what he called his 'felicific calculus' he set out guidelines for making comparisons between pleasures, taking into account such features as their intensity, duration, tendency to give rise to further pleasures, and so on. He was even prepared to include animals in the sums. To do so, however, raises very serious difficulties of the weighting of the pleasures and pains of different species and different individual animals, assuming, of course, that we could come up with an accurate measure of these. How are we to assess the pleasure of a python slowly devouring a small antelope alive against the pain felt by the antelope? Or what about the mosquito's pleasure felt at the expense of its victim's minor irritation?

Mill found Bentham's approach crude: in place of it he suggested a distinction between so-called higher and lower pleasures. He argued that anyone who had truly experienced the higher pleasures, which were, in his view, mainly intellectual, would automatically prefer them to the so-called lower ones, which were primarily physical. In Mill's scheme, higher pleasures counted for more in the calculation of happiness than did lower ones: in other words he assessed pleasures according to their quality as well as their quantity. He argued that it would certainly be preferable to be a sad but wise Socrates than to be a happy but ignorant fool, on the grounds that Socrates' pleasures would be of a higher kind than the fool's.

But this sounds elitist. It is an intellectual's justification for his own particular preferences and the interests and values of his social class. The fact remains that relative amounts of happiness are extremely difficult to calculate. And indeed this problem would still not be completely resolved even if we were to accept Mill's division between higher and lower pleasures.

A more basic difficulty of calculation occurs in deciding what are to count as the effects of any particular action. If someone hit a child because the child had misbehaved, the question of whether or not this was a moral action would depend entirely upon the consequences of the action. But are we to count only the immediate effects of hitting the child, or must we take into account the long-term effects? If the latter, then we may end up trying to balance such things as the child's emotional development, and possibly even the effects on the child's own children, against the child's happiness derived from avoidance of potentially dangerous situations as a result of the punishment training. With any action the effects can stretch far into the future, and there is rarely an obvious cut-off point.

PROBLEM CASES

A further objection to utilitarianism is that it can justify many actions which are usually thought immoral. For instance, if it could be shown that publicly hanging someone who is innocent would have the direct beneficial effect of reducing violent crime by acting as a deterrent, and so, overall, cause more pleasure than pain, then a utilitarian would be obliged to say that hanging the innocent person was the morally right thing to do. But such a conclusion is repugnant to our sense of justice. Of course a feeling of repugnance towards some of its conclusions doesn't prove that there is something wrong with the theory of utilitarianism. A hard-line utilitarian would presumably quite happily stomach the conclusion. However, such unpalatable consequences should make us wary about accepting utilitarianism as a completely satisfactory moral theory.

Utilitarians like Bentham, who believe that happiness is simply a blissful state of mind, leave themselves open to a further objection.

Their theory suggests that the world would be a morally better place if a mood-altering drug such as ecstasy were secretly added to the water supply, provided that it increased the total pleasure. Yet most of us would feel that a life with fewer blissful moments but the choice of how we achieve them would be preferable to this, and that the person who added the drug to the water supply would have done something immoral.

A related point has sometimes been made using the thought experiment of the Experience Machine, an example thought up by Robert Nozick (1938–2002). Imagine that you have the option of being plugged into a sophisticated virtual reality machine that will give you the illusion of having whatever experiences you most desire. You only have the choice of being plugged in for life; however, once you have been plugged in, you won't realize that you are plugged in. This machine could give you a huge range of blissful mental states, yet most people considering this imaginary situation say they wouldn't opt for it. They wouldn't seek their own happiness irrespective of how it is produced: this suggests that happiness is not just a matter of mental states, but includes a notion of how those states are produced. And it is not at all plausible to suggest that a world in which everyone was plugged into Experience Machines giving them pleasant experiences would be morally superior to the present one. Yet on Bentham's view it would have to be, since for him the methods of producing the blissful mental states did not matter.

Consider another difficult case for the utilitarian. Whereas Kant says that we ought to keep our promises whatever the consequences of doing so, utilitarians would calculate the probable happiness that would arise from keeping or breaking promises in each case, and act accordingly. Utilitarians might well conclude that, in cases where they knew that their creditors had forgotten about a debt and wouldn't be likely ever to remember it, it would be morally right not to pay back money which they had borrowed. The borrowers' increased happiness due to increased wealth might well outweigh any unhappiness they felt about deceiving others. And the creditors would, presumably, experience little or no unhappiness as they would have forgotten about the debt.

But in such cases personal integrity seems to be an important aspect of human interaction. Indeed, many would see telling the truth, repaying debts, being honest in our dealings with other people, and so on, as central examples of moral behaviour. For such people, utilitarianism, with its rejection of the concept of absolute duties, is inadequate as a moral theory.

NEGATIVE UTILITARIANISM

Utilitarianism is based on the assumption that the right action in any circumstances is the one which produces the greatest overall happiness. But perhaps this puts too much stress on happiness. The avoidance of pain and suffering is a far more important goal than the achievement of a balance of happiness over unhappiness. Surely a world in which no one was particularly happy, but no one suffered extreme pain, would be more appealing than one in which some people suffered extremes of unhappiness, but these were balanced out by many people experiencing great contentment and happiness?

One way of meeting this objection is to modify utilitarianism into what is usually known as negative utilitarianism. The basic principle of negative utilitarianism is that the best action in any circumstances is not the one which produces the greatest balance of happiness over unhappiness for the greatest number of people, but the one which produces the least overall amount of unhappiness. For instance, a rich negative utilitarian might wonder whether to leave all his or her money to one poor and severely ill person who was in great pain and whose suffering would be relieved considerably by this gift, or else to divide it between a thousand moderately happy people, who would each increase their happiness a little because of this gift. An ordinary utilitarian would calculate which action would produce the greater balance of pleasure over pain for the greatest number of people; a negative utilitarian would only be concerned to minimize suffering. So, whilst an ordinary utilitarian would probably divide the money between the thousand moderately happy people, because that would maximize happiness, the negative utilitarian would leave the money to the severely ill person, thereby minimizing suffering.

Such negative utilitarianism is, however, still open to many of the difficulties of calculation that arise for ordinary utilitarianism. It is also open to a criticism of its own.

CRITICISM OF NEGATIVE UTILITARIANISM

DESTRUCTION OF ALL LIFE

The best way to eliminate all suffering in the world would be to eliminate all sentient life. If there were no living things capable of feeling pain, then there would be no pain. If it were possible to do this in a painless way, perhaps by means of a huge atomic explosion, then, by the principle of negative utilitarianism, this would be the morally right action. Even if a certain amount of pain were involved in the process, the long-term benefits in pain elimination would probably outweigh it. Yet this conclusion is hardly acceptable. At the very least negative utilitarianism needs to be reformulated so as to avoid it.

RULE UTILITARIANISM

As a way of getting round the objection that ordinary utilitarianism (also known as act utilitarianism) has many unpalatable consequences, some philosophers have suggested another modified version of the theory, known as rule utilitarianism. This is supposed to combine the best aspects of act utilitarianism with the best of deontological ethics.

Rule utilitarians, rather than assessing the consequences of each action separately, adopt general rules about the kinds of action which tend to produce greater happiness for the greatest number of people. For instance, because in general punishing innocent people produces more unhappiness than happiness, rule utilitarians would adopt the rule 'never punish the innocent', even though there may be particular instances in which punishing the innocent would produce more happiness than unhappiness – such as when it acts as an effective deterrent against violent crime. Similarly, a rule utilitarian would advocate keeping promises because in general this produces a balance of happiness over unhappiness.

Rule utilitarianism has the great practical benefit that it makes it unnecessary to perform a complicated calculation every time you are faced with having to make a moral decision. However, in a situation in which you know that greater happiness will result from breaking a promise than from keeping it, and, given that your basic moral sympathies lie with a utilitarian outlook, it seems perverse to stick to the rule rather than to treat the individual case on its merits.

VIRTUE THEORY

Virtue theory is largely based on Aristotle's *Nicomachean Ethics* and as a result is sometimes known as neo-Aristotelianism ('neo' meaning 'new'). Unlike Kantians and utilitarians, who typically concentrate on the rightness or wrongness of particular actions, virtue theorists focus on character and are interested in the individual's life as a whole. The central question for virtue theorists is 'How should I live?' The answer they give to this question is: cultivate the virtues. It is only by cultivating the virtues that you will flourish as a human being.

FLOURISHING

According to Aristotle, everyone wants to flourish. The Greek word he used for flourishing was *eudaimonia*. This is sometimes translated as 'happiness', but this translation can be confusing since Aristotle believed that you could experience, for instance, great physical pleasure without achieving *eudaimonia*. *Eudaimonia* applies to a whole life, not just to particular states you might find yourself in from hour to hour. Perhaps 'true happiness' would be a better translation; but this makes it sound as if *eudaimonia* were a blissful mental state at which you arrive, rather than a way of living your life successfully. Aristotle believed that certain ways of living promote human flourishing, just as certain ways of caring for a cherry tree will lead it to grow, blossom, and fruit.

THE VIRTUES

Aristotle claimed that cultivating the virtues is the way to flourish as a human being. But what is a virtue? It is a pattern of behaviour and feeling: a tendency to act, desire, and feel in particular ways in appropriate situations. Unlike Kant, Aristotle thought that experiencing appropriate emotions was central to the art of leading a good life. A virtue isn't an unthinking habit, but rather involves an intelligent judgement about the appropriate response to the situation you are in.

Someone who has the virtue of being generous would, in appropriate situations, feel and act in a generous way. This would involve the judgement that the situation and response were of an appropriate kind. If put in the situation of the Good Samaritan, a virtuous person would both feel compassion for the man left by the roadside, and act in a charitable way towards him. A Samaritan who only helped the victim because he had calculated some future benefit for himself would not be acting virtuously, since generosity involves giving without thought of benefit to yourself.

If the Samaritan had arrived at the time the robbers were attacking their unfortunate victim, and the Samaritan had had the virtue of courage, then he would have overcome any fear and confronted the robbers. Part of what being courageous means is having the ability to overcome fear.

Virtues such as generosity and courage are, virtue theorists believe, traits which any human being will need in order to live well. This might sound as if a virtuous individual could pick and choose from a portfolio of virtues those which he or she wanted to develop, or as if someone who possessed a single virtue to a great degree could be a virtuous person. However, this would be a mis-understanding. For Aristotle, the virtuous person is someone who has harmonized all the virtues: they must be woven into the fabric of the virtuous person's life.

CRITICISMS OF VIRTUE THEORY

WHICH VIRTUES SHOULD WE ADOPT?

A major difficulty with virtue theory is establishing which patterns of behaviour, desire, and feeling are to count as virtues. The virtue theorist's answer is: those which a human needs in order to flourish. But this doesn't really give much help. Virtue theorists often produce lists of virtues such as benevolence, honesty, courage, generosity, and loyalty, and so on. They also analyse these in some detail. But, as there is not complete overlap between their lists, there is room for debate about what should be included. And it is not always clear on what grounds something gets designated a virtue.

The danger is that virtue theorists simply redefine their prejudices and preferred ways of life as virtues, and the activities they dislike as vices. Someone who likes fine food and wine might declare that subtle stimulation of the taste buds is an essential part of living well as a human being, and thus that being a lover of fine food and wine is a virtue. A monogamist might declare fidelity to one sexual partner a virtue; a sexually promiscuous virtue theorist might make a case for the virtue of sexual independence. Thus virtue theory can be used as an intellectual smokescreen behind which prejudices are smuggled in. What is more, if the virtue theorist opts for accepting only those ways of behaving, desiring, and feeling which are typically considered virtuous in a particular society, then the theory emerges as an essentially conservative one, with little scope for changing that society on moral grounds.

HUMAN NATURE

A further criticism of virtue theory is that it presupposes that there is such a thing as human nature and so that there are some general patterns of behaviour and feeling appropriate for all human beings. However, such a view has been challenged by many philosophers, who believe that it is a serious mistake to assume that human nature exists. I will return to this topic in the section on naturalism below.

A further assumption that virtue theorists make is that individuals' characteristics are relatively stable, that, for example, someone who is generous is reliably generous across a range of circumstances. Yet recent psychological research suggests that we are far more affected by circumstances than we believe we are − aspects of our environment significantly affect our behaviour without our realizing that this is going on. For example, people tend to be far more generous when outside a bakery smelling fresh bread than they are when standing outside a hardware store. If our behaviour is so easily affected by such circumstances, this casts some doubt on whether the virtuous person whom virtue theorists praise so highly is a realistic possibility. We may all of us be far more creatures of our circumstances than is generally realized, and this makes the notion of fixed virtues less secure as the foundation of morality than most virtue theorists believe it to be.

APPLIED ETHICS

So far in this chapter I have outlined three basic types of ethical theory. Obviously these are not the only types of ethical theory, but they are the most important ones. Now let's look at how philosophers actually apply their theories to real rather than imagined moral decisions. This is known as practical or applied ethics. In order to illustrate the sorts of considerations which are relevant in applied ethics, we will focus on one ethical issue, namely that of euthanasia or mercy killing.

EUTHANASIA

Euthanasia is usually defined as mercy killing. The issue of whether or not euthanasia is justified typically arises with the very old and the chronically sick, particularly those in great pain. If, for instance, someone is in pain, and has no prospect of living a worthwhile life, is it morally acceptable to switch off their life-support machine or, perhaps, even administer a lethal drug? This is a practical ethical question, one which doctors are frequently obliged to address.

As with most applied ethics, the philosophical questions which arise in relation to euthanasia are not all ethical ones. To begin with, there are a number of important distinctions which we can make between types of euthanasia. First, there is voluntary euthanasia – when the patient wishes to die, and expresses this wish. This is usually a form of assisted suicide. Second, there is involuntary euthanasia – when the patient does not wish to die, but this wish is ignored. This is equivalent to murder in many, though not all, cases. Third, there is non-voluntary euthanasia – when the patient is unconscious, or in no position to express a wish. Here we will concentrate on the issue of the morality of voluntary euthanasia.

The general ethical theory that an individual adopts obviously determines their response to particular questions. So a Christian who accepts the duty-based ethical theory outlined at the beginning of this chapter is likely to answer questions about euthanasia in a different way from someone who accepts John Stuart Mill's consequentialist theory, utilitarianism. A Christian would probably have doubts about the moral justification of voluntary euthanasia because it would seem to contradict the Commandment 'Thou shalt not kill'. However, it might not be as simple as this. There could be a conflict between this Commandment and the New Testament Commandment to love one's neighbour. If someone is in great pain, and wants to die, it can be an act of love to help them end their life. A Christian would have to decide which of these two Commandments had more force, and act accordingly.

Similarly, someone who adopted Kant's ethical theory might feel duty-bound never to kill. To kill someone would seem to go against Kant's view that we should treat other people as ends in themselves and never as means to an end, and respect their humanity. But this same version of the Categorical Imperative could, in the case of voluntary euthanasia, provide a moral justification *for* ending someone's life, if that is what the patient wants and yet is unable to do it unaided.

A utilitarian would see the issue in a very different light. For a utilitarian, the difficulty would not be a conflict of duties, but rather how to calculate the effects of the various possible courses of action available. Whichever course of action would cause the greatest amount of happiness for the most people, or at least the greatest balance of happiness over unhappiness, would be the morally right one. The utilitarian would consider the consequences for the patient. If the patient were to carry on living, he or she would experience great pain, and probably die very soon anyway. If the patient were to die through an act of euthanasia, then pain would cease, as would all capacity for happiness. However, these are not the only effects to take into consideration. There are a number of side-effects. For instance, the death of the patient by euthanasia might cause distress to the patient's relatives. Also, the act of euthanasia might involve breaking the law, and so the person who helped the patient to die might run the risk of prosecution. This also raises questions of the morality of law-breaking in general.

Another side-effect of performing a single act of euthanasia is that it might make it easier for unscrupulous doctors to kill patients under the guise of it being the wishes of the patient. Opponents of all euthanasia often point out that Hitler's extermination techniques were first tried out on victims of an involuntary euthanasia programme. Perhaps every individual act of voluntary euthanasia makes it easier for someone to bring in a policy of involuntary euthanasia. A utilitarian would weigh up such possible consequences of action in order to decide whether the particular act of euthanasia were morally justified.

A virtue theorist would approach the issue of euthanasia somewhat differently, emphasizing the character of the person performing the act of euthanasia. Although killing another person is usually contrary both to the virtue of justice and to that of charity, in the special case of voluntary euthanasia, when death would clearly benefit the other person, the virtue of charity would permit it. However, even in this case the virtue of justice might still oppose it. A virtue theorist would not lay down rigid rules of behaviour, but would be sensitive to the details of the particular case.

As this brief discussion of a practical ethical problem illustrates, there are rarely easy answers about what we should do. And yet frequently we are forced to make moral judgements. Contemporary developments in technology and genetics are constantly giving rise to new ethical questions about life and death. In medical science, the development of the possibility of *in vitro* fertilization, and of genetic engineering, poses difficult ethical questions, as do technological breakthroughs, such as those in the field of computer science which permit surveillance and access to personal information on an undreamed-of scale. The AIDS epidemic has brought with it a wide range of ethical questions about when it is acceptable to force someone to be tested for the HIV virus. Clarification of the possible approaches to such problems can only be useful. Often the most helpful philosophical contribution to genuine moral discussion does not take the form of the application of a moral theory. Philosophers can be good at spotting reasoning errors in such discussion, errors that turn on logical rather than moral points. But the fact remains that ethical decisions are the most difficult and the most important that we make. The responsibility for our choices ultimately rests with each of us.

ETHICS AND META-ETHICS

The three types of ethical theory we have examined so far – duty-based, consequentialist, and virtue theory – are examples of first-order theories. That is, they are theories about how we should behave. Moral philosophers are also interested in second-order questions: these are questions not about what we ought to do but about the status of ethical theories. This theorizing about ethical theories is usually known as meta-ethics. A typical meta-ethical question is 'What is the meaning of "right" in the moral context?' I will consider three examples of meta-ethical theories here: ethical naturalism, moral relativism, and emotivism.

NATURALISM

One of the most widely discussed meta-ethical questions in the twentieth century was that of whether or not so-called naturalistic ethical theories are acceptable. A naturalistic ethical theory is one which is based on the assumption that ethical judgements follow directly from scientifically discoverable facts – often facts about human nature.

Utilitarian ethics moves from a description of human nature to a view of how we ought to behave. Ideally, utilitarianism would use a scientific measurement of the quality and quantity of each person's happiness in order to demonstrate what is right and wrong. In contrast, Kantian ethics are not so closely linked to human psychology: our categorical duties supposedly follow from logical, not psychological, considerations.

CRITICISMS OF NATURALISM

FACT/VALUE DISTINCTION

Many philosophers believe that all naturalistic ethical theories are based on a mistake: the failure to recognize that facts and values are fundamentally different sorts of things. Those opposed to naturalism – anti-naturalists – argue that no factual description ever leads automatically to any value judgement: further argument is always needed. This is sometimes known as Hume's Law, after David Hume, who was one of the first to point out that moral philosophers often move from discussions of 'what is' to discussions of 'what ought to be' without further argument.

Anti-naturalists claim that the further argument needed to move smoothly from facts to value, or, as it is sometimes put, from 'is' to 'ought', is impossible to give. Fact and value are different realms and there is no logical connection between, say, human happiness and moral worth. Following G. E. Moore (1873–1958), anti-naturalists sometimes use the term the Naturalistic Fallacy to describe the alleged mistake of arguing from facts to value, a fallacy being a type of bad argument.

One argument anti-naturalists use to support their position is known as the Open Question Argument.

THE OPEN QUESTION ARGUMENT

This argument, first used by G. E. Moore, is really just a way of making clearer people's existing beliefs about ethics. It is a way of showing that most of us, in the way that we think about such moral terms as 'good' or 'right', have already rejected the naturalistic approach.

The argument is this. First, take any statement of fact from which ethical conclusions are supposed to follow. For instance, it may have been a fact that, of all the choices available to the Good Samaritan, helping the robbed man was the one that would cause the most happiness for the greatest number of people. On a utilitarian analysis – which is a form of ethical naturalism – it would logically follow that helping the man would therefore be a morally good action. However, an anti-naturalist using the Open Question Argument would point out that there is nothing logically inconsistent in saying 'This action is likely to give rise to the most happiness for the greater number of people, but is it the morally right thing to do?' If this version of naturalism were true, it would not be worth asking such a question: the answer would be obvious. As it is, the anti-naturalists argue, it remains an open question.

An anti-naturalist would claim that the same sort of question could be asked about any situation in which a description of natural qualities is supposed to give rise automatically to an ethical conclusion. The Open Question Argument is one way in which anti-naturalists give support to their slogan 'No "ought" from "is"'.

The Open Question Argument doesn't conclusively prove that you can't derive an 'ought' from an 'is', however. Several philosophers have pointed to the existence of social practices which suggest that this transition can be made. For example, if I promise to pay you ten pounds, it is a fact that I speak the words 'I promise to pay you ten pounds' and if I do this sincerely it puts me under a moral obligation to pay you ten pounds. This seems to be a counter-example to the claim that you cannot derive an 'ought' from an 'is'.

NO HUMAN NATURE

Other philosophers, such as Jean-Paul Sartre (1905–80) in his lecture *Existentialism and Humanism*, have attacked naturalistic ethics (at least the kind that says that morality is determined by facts about human nature) from a different angle. They have argued that it is a mistake to assume, as virtue theory does, that there is such a thing as human nature. This, they say, is a form of self-deception, a denial of the great responsibility each of us has. We all have to choose our values for ourselves, and there is no simple answer to ethical questions. We cannot work out what we should do from a scientific description of the way the world is; but nevertheless we are all forced to make ethical decisions. It is an aspect of the human condition that we have to make these value judgements, but without any firm guidelines from outside ourselves. Naturalism in ethics is a self-deceptive denial of this freedom to choose for ourselves.

MORAL RELATIVISM

It is uncontroversially true that people in different societies have different customs and different ideas about right and wrong. There is no world consensus on which actions are right and wrong, even though there is a considerable overlap between views on this. If we consider how much moral views have changed both from place to place and from age to age it can be tempting to think that there are no absolute moral facts, but rather that morality is always relative to the society in which you have been brought up. On such a view, since slavery was morally acceptable to most Ancient Greeks but is not to most Europeans today, slavery was right for the Ancient Greeks but would be wrong for today's Europeans. This view, known as moral relativism, makes morality simply a description of the values held by a particular society at a particular time. This is a meta-ethical view about the nature of moral judgements. Moral judgements can only be judged true or false relative to a particular society. There are no absolute moral judgements: they are all relative. Moral relativism contrasts starkly with the view that some actions are absolutely right or wrong, a view held, for instance, by many who believe that morality consists of God's commands to humanity.

Relativists often couple this account of morality with the belief that, because morality is relative, we should never interfere with the customs of other societies on the grounds that there is no neutral standpoint from which to judge. This view has been especially popular with anthropologists, perhaps partly because they have often seen at first hand the destruction wreaked on other societies by a crude importation of Western values. When moral relativism has this added component, indicating how we should behave towards other societies, it is usually known as normative relativism.

CRITICISMS OF MORAL RELATIVISM

ARE RELATIVISTS INCONSISTENT?

Moral relativists are sometimes accused of inconsistency since they claim that all moral judgements are relative but at the same time want us to believe that the theory of moral relativism is itself *absolutely* true. This is only a serious problem for a moral relativist who is also a relativist about truth, that is, someone who believes that there is no such thing as absolute truth, only truths relative to particular societies. That sort of relativist can't hold that any theory at all is *absolutely* true.

Nevertheless normative relativists are certainly open to the charge of inconsistency. They believe both that all moral judgements are relative to your society *and* that societies shouldn't interfere with each other. Yet this second belief is surely an example of an absolute moral judgement, one that is completely incompatible with the basic premise of normative relativism. This is a damning criticism of normative relativism.

WHAT COUNTS AS A SOCIETY?

Moral relativists are usually vague about what is to count as a society. For instance, within contemporary Britain there are certainly members of subcultures who believe that it is morally acceptable to use banned drugs for recreational purposes. At what point will a relativist be prepared to say that the members of these subcultures form a separate society, and so can be said to have their own morality which is immune to criticism from other cultures? There is no obvious answer to this question.

NO MORAL CRITICISM OF A SOCIETY'S VALUES

Even if the previous criticism can be met, a further difficulty with moral relativism arises. It doesn't seem to leave open the possibility of moral criticism of the central values of a society. If moral judgements are defined in terms of that society's central values, no critic of these central values can use *moral* arguments against them. In a society in which the dominant view is that women shouldn't be allowed to vote, anyone advocating enfranchisement for women would be suggesting something immoral relative to the values of that society.

EMOTIVISM

Another important meta-ethical theory is known as emotivism or non-cognitivism. Emotivists, such as A. J. Ayer (1910–88) in Chapter 6 of his *Language, Truth and Logic*, claim that all ethical statements are literally meaningless. They do not express any facts at all; what they express is the speaker's emotion. Moral judgements have no literal meaning at all: they are just expressions of emotion, like grunts, sighs, or laughter.

So when someone says 'Torture is wrong' or 'You ought to tell the truth', they are doing little more than showing how they feel about torture or truth-telling. What they say is neither true nor false: it is more or less the same as shouting 'Boo!' at the mention of torture, or 'Hooray!' at the mention of truth-telling. Indeed, emotivism has sometimes been called the Boo/Hooray theory. Just as when someone shouts 'Boo!' or 'Hooray!', they are not simply showing how they feel, but usually also trying to encourage other people to share their feeling, so with moral statements the speaker is often attempting to persuade someone to think likewise about the issue.

CRITICISMS OF EMOTIVISM

MORAL ARGUMENT IMPOSSIBLE

One criticism of emotivism is that if it were true then all moral argument would be impossible. The closest we would be able to get to moral argument would be two people expressing their emotions to each other: the equivalent of one shouting 'Boo!' and the other 'Hooray!' But, it is alleged, we do have serious debates on moral issues, so emotivism must be false.

However, an emotivist would not see this criticism as any threat to the theory. Many different sorts of arguments are used in so-called moral debates. For instance, in discussing the practical ethical question of whether or not abortion on demand is morally acceptable, what is at issue may in part be a factual matter. It may be a question of the age at which a foetus would be able to survive outside the womb that is being argued about. This would be a scientific rather than an ethical question. Or else people apparently engaged in ethical debate may be concerned with the definition of ethical terms such as 'right', 'wrong', 'responsibility', and so on: the emotivist would allow that such a debate can be meaningful. It is only actual moral judgements such as 'Killing people is wrong' that are merely expressions of emotion.

So an emotivist would agree that some meaningful debate about moral issues does actually occur: it is only when the participants make actual moral judgements that the discussion becomes a meaningless expression of emotion.

DANGEROUS CONSEQUENCES

A second criticism of emotivism is that even if it is true, it is likely to have dangerous consequences. If everybody came to believe that a statement such as 'Murder is wrong' was the equivalent of saying 'Murder – yuk!', then, it is claimed, society would collapse.

A view, such as the Kantian one, that moral judgements apply to everyone – that they are impersonal – gives good reasons for individuals keeping to a generally accepted moral code. But if all that we are doing when we make a moral judgement is expressing our emotions, then it does not seem to matter very much which moral judgements we choose to make: we might just as well say 'Torturing little children is right', if that is our feeling. And no one can engage in significant moral argument with us about this judgement. The best that they can do is express their own moral feelings on the matter.

However, this isn't really an argument against emotivism since it does not directly challenge the theory: it is just an indication of the dangers to society of emotivism being widely accepted as true, which is a separate issue.

CONCLUSION

As can be seen from this brief discussion, moral philosophy is a vast and complicated area of philosophy. Post-war British and American philosophers have tended to focus on meta-ethical questions. However, in recent years they have been turning their attention more towards practical ethical problems such as the morality of euthanasia, abortion, embryo research, animal experiments, and many other topics. Whilst philosophy does not give easy answers to these or any moral questions, it does provide a vocabulary and a framework within which such questions can be intelligently discussed.

FURTHER READING

James Rachels's *The Elements of Moral Philosophy* (4th edition, Boston, Mass.: McGraw-Hill, 2003) is an excellent short introduction to ethics. Another good book in this area is Simon Blackburn's *Ethics: A Very Short Introduction* (Oxford: Oxford University Press, 2003), originally published under the title *Being Good* (Oxford: Oxford University Press, 2002).

Richard Norman's *The Moral Philosophers* (2nd edition, Oxford: Clarendon Press, 1998) is a very good introduction to the history of ethics: it includes detailed suggestions for reading.

The best introduction to utilitarianism is *Utilitarianism and its Critics*, edited by Jonathan Glover (New York: Macmillan, 1990). This includes excerpts from Bentham's and Mill's most important writing as well as more recent work on utilitarianism and its variants. Some of the material is quite advanced, but Glover's introductions to each section are very helpful. Roger Crisp's *Mill on Utilitarianism* (London: Routledge, Routledge Guidebook series, 1997) is another outstanding book in this area. J. J. C. Smart and Bernard Williams's *Utilitarianism: For and Against* (Cambridge: Cambridge University Press, 1973) is a classic discussion of utilitarianism.

On the subject of applied ethics, Jonathan Glover's *Causing Death and Saving Lives* (London: Penguin, 1977) and Peter Singer's *Practical Ethics* (3rd edition, Cambridge: Cambridge University Press, 2011) are both interesting and accessible. *Applied Ethics* (Oxford: Oxford University Press, 1986), edited by Peter Singer, is an excellent selection of essays. *A Companion to Ethics*, also edited by Peter Singer (Oxford: Blackwell, 1991), is a more substantial introduction to a wide range of topics within ethics. Michael Sandel's *Justice: What's The Right Thing to Do?* (London: Allen Lane, 2009), is a very readable, wide-ranging book about morality in which the author rejects utilitarian approaches in favour of a form of Aristotelianism, using real-life cases to support his views. Anne Thomson's *Critical Reasoning in Ethics* (London: Routledge, 1999) is a very useful guide to the application of critical thinking to ethical issues.

J. L. Mackie's *Ethics: Inventing Right and Wrong* (London: Penguin, 1977) and G. J. Warnock's *Contemporary Moral Philosophy* (London: Macmillan, 1967) are introductory books on moral philosophy well worth reading, though neither of them is easy.

ANIMALS

Since ancient times philosophers have asked questions about how human beings differ from other animals. Vegetarianism on moral grounds is not a new phenomenon: some Ancient Greeks refused to eat meat. Nevertheless, for several thousand years, the dominant view has been that animals are there for humans to do with as we see fit – and that includes killing them to eat, making clothes and shoes out of their skins, using them in scientific and commercial research, and even in entertainment such as in recreational fishing, some forms of hunting, circuses and bullfighting. However, since the late twentieth century there has been a significant philosophical interest in questions about animal experience, and how we should treat non-humans. Questions of animal welfare are increasingly seen as pressing moral issues, not simply practical questions about farming or scientific methodology.

ANIMAL SUFFERING

It does not take much imagination to realize that a mammal, such as a dog or a cat, a bull, or a chimpanzee is capable of feeling pain and that it is unpleasant for them. These animals all squeal, take avoidance action, and show many of the signs of distress at physical harm. Obviously, unlike most humans, they can't tell us about their experience in language (with the possible exception, perhaps, of a few chimpanzees who have been taught a basic sign language), but by far the most plausible explanation of their behaviour is that they feel pain more or less as we do.

A starting point for discussion of how we ought to treat animals, then, is an acknowledgement that most, and possibly all, are capable of feeling pain. They differ in this respect from inanimate objects, such as tables, stones, and cars; they also differ in this respect from plants, which lack a nervous system. Very few people would deny this basic starting point, but historically at least one important philosopher, René Descartes, did exactly that.

CRITICISM OF ANIMAL SUFFERING VIEW

'ANIMALS DON'T FEEL PAIN'

Like a number of his contemporaries, Descartes believed that human beings were fundamentally different from other animals. Human beings, he maintained, have a soul that interacts with the physical body. Unfortunately he did not believe that other animals had souls. Their apparent experience of pain could be explained by mechanics. Human bodies and animal bodies were, he thought, quite similar in that they operated like machines. The difference between the two was that, whereas human 'machines' were steered by the soul that interacted with the body, animals, in his view, were mere machines. So a dog that squealed when its paw was trapped was simply like a machine with an alarm bell ringing. The squeal wasn't an indication of actual experience of pain. This meant that he had no qualms about performing vivisection of animals – dissections while the animals were still alive – in order to advance science. He would have argued that to perform a vivisection on a human being would be a moral outrage, because the soul would have been capable of experiencing great suffering. But to do the same to an animal, he thought, was not morally wrong.

CRITICISM OF DESCARTES ON ANIMAL PAIN

BASED ON AN IMPLAUSIBLE THEORY

Descartes's view about animal pain was based on an implausible theory about the nature of the mind as a kind of 'ghost' in the 'machine' of the body (this view, Cartesian dualism, is discussed and criticized in pp. 140–42).

For those who believe in some form of physicalism (see p. 143 for more about physicalism), the notion that the mind and experience are not just dependent on having a body, but are experienced by the body, it is highly implausible and disturbing that anyone should think that animals are incapable of feeling pain, given how similar their nervous systems are to ours. But even mind/body dualists can recognize that animals feel pain if they believe that animals have minds.

DARWINISM EXPLAINS SIMILARITIES WITH OTHER ANIMALS

Fortunately very few people are likely to argue that animals are incapable of feeling pain. Charles Darwin's theory of evolution has been important in explaining how human beings probably evolved from other animals, and stressing the close connections between humans and other animals. Before Darwin's ideas became widely accepted it was more common to think of human beings as radically different in kind from other animals.

Nevertheless, some people do persist in believing that animal suffering is very different from human suffering, principally because non human animals, lacking language, are incapable of thinking about their own actual and potential pain in the ways that we do. However, there is still the issue for such thinkers that humans who have yet to learn language or have no language, perhaps due to having had a severe stroke or other brain damage, will be in more or less the same position as these non-human animals.

THE RELEVANCE OF ANIMAL SUFFERING

Given that animals, particularly mammals with nervous systems that are not importantly different from human nervous systems, clearly do feel and dislike pain, what follows? Jeremy Bentham (see Chapter 2) argued that the suffering of animals should be included in any moral assessment of how we should behave. His utilitarianism was based on the idea that we ought to maximize pleasure and minimize pain. Since animals can feel pain, their pain should be included in the 'felicific calculus', the calculation of the likely pleasure and pain arising from any prospective action.

However, as Bentham realized, most human beings are capable of different sorts of pleasure and pain from other animals. If we focus on the experience of pain, through language we are able to communicate and anticipate likely outcomes of actions in different ways from other animals. This means that a human being who is, for example, in a prison cell awaiting torture, would probably experience more intense psychological suffering than an animal in a similar position because the human would be able to anticipate the pain. This would make the overall quantity of pain higher in the case of a human being in this situation than it would an animal similarly placed.

This does not mean that animal suffering doesn't count, only that the suffering may have a different intensity, duration, and effects on others – all consequences that need to be given weight in a calculation of the pleasure or pain that results from a course of action. From this angle, some utilitarians have argued that there is nothing morally wrong with eating other animals if they have been reared humanely, and if they have been slaughtered in ways that cause them minimal suffering. The pleasures of human beings eating meat have to be weighed against the overall suffering of the animals in the process of rearing and slaughtering them. If the pleasures of the human beings outweigh the suffering of the animals, on this simple calculation meat-eating may be justified. This was in fact Bentham's own position.

ANIMAL WELFARE

However, in reality, large-scale farming frequently fails to guarantee animal welfare. In some countries so-called 'factory farming' is tolerated, when animals such as pigs, calves, hens, cattle – all clearly capable of suffering – are kept in very confined and crowded conditions, and treated as simply the means to produce meat, eggs, or dairy produce at the lowest possible price, with negligible concern for the pain endured by the animals. It is unlikely that any utilitarian calculation could justify such practices.

SPECIESISM

The contemporary Australian philosopher Peter Singer (1946–), amongst others, has claimed that treating animals' interests differently from those of human beings is 'speciesism' (a term coined by Richard Ryder). Speciesism is a bit like racism. It is a form of prejudiced discrimination on non-relevant grounds and is something to be avoided and condemned as vigorously as racism is. Racists don't usually take the interests of members of the group they oppress as relevant to their actions. They are typically content to cause suffering to some racial groups because they believe that they are somehow inferior to the racists' racial group.

Speciesism, like racism, involves thinking that the interests of others don't really count for anything, or at least not very much, but in this case the 'others' are non-human animals. Speciesism takes the species as the defining feature of moral worth, not the capacity of the individual concerned to have interests. It is, anti-speciesists argue, an irrational bias in favour of your own kind.

It is important to realize that those who are opposed to speciesism aren't arguing that we should treat all animals in exactly the same way. The point is that we give equal consideration to their interests on the grounds that non-human animals are subjects of lives that are lived and experienced. This will often mean, when the interests of a non-human animal come into conflict with a human that an anti-speciesist will still give preference to the human. But this won't be based merely on the human being's status as a member of the species *homo sapiens*; rather, it will be on account of a human's greater capacity for certain kinds of psychological suffering, for example.

ARGUMENTS FOR SPECIESISM

ANIMALS EXIST FOR HUMAN BENEFIT

'Speciesism' is not a neutral term. It implies strong disapproval. But some Christians argue that God gave human beings dominion over other animals, and so we have a God-given right to treat non-human animals differently from humans: it is in part what God put animals there for. In other words, some Christians claim that there is a scriptural justification for their speciesism, and that it is justified as part of God's plan for humanity. This view has been held by many non-Christians too: for example, it was Aristotle's view that other animals exist for the sake of human beings – they're there as beasts of burden, as potential food and transport, and their skins make excellent clothes and shoes.

ANIMALS DON'T SHOW RESPECT FOR EACH OTHER

Another argument that speciesists sometimes use in defence of their position is that animals clearly don't show each other much respect since many of them hunt, kill, and eat each other. Killer whales eat baby seals, so why should we be concerned about harming killer whales? If animals harm, kill, and eat each other, the argument goes, then why shouldn't we do it to them?

One response to this is that non-human animals aren't in a position to think this sort of thing through, consider the options, and make a rational choice. We, however, can do this, so we should. Furthermore, anti-speciesists can point out, human beings don't need to eat meat or fish: we can survive well without either; whereas many animals have no choice in this matter. Some people argue, on the basis of medical evidence, that a well-balanced vegetarian diet is significantly healthier for human beings than one that includes meat. A healthier life is likely to be one of greater happiness and less pain, and one that will make fewer demands on scarce communal health resources, so perhaps there are even utilitarian reasons for preferring vegetarianism above meat. This argument is sometimes combined with the ecological one, namely that growing crops is far more efficient than rearing animals and produces far less CO_2, thereby benefiting everyone.

THE ANALOGY WITH FAVOURING OUR OWN CHILDREN

A further argument that some thinkers use in favour of speciesism rests on an analogy with parents' biases towards their own children's interests when these come into conflict with others' interests. So, for example, a mother may want her child to succeed in a job interview, even though this means that other candidates will fail to get the job. This sort of preference for our own children feels right: we might be concerned about a parent who was always prepared to see the merits of other children above his or her own. If you accept that such an exaggerated concern for the interests of our own offspring is morally acceptable and perhaps even required, then you might be prepared to accept the view that the same sort of reasoning applies by analogy to members of our own species. The argument is that we are morally justified in treating members of our own species like members of our extended family (which in a sense they are), and so giving them special treatment relative to other animals.

ANTI-SPECIESISM

Anti-speciesism is based on the idea that non-human animals, particularly mammals, clearly do have interests. Unlike, for example, a stone, a mouse has an interest in not being hurt, and a chimpanzee has an interest in not being experimented on. We know that a mouse will suffer if its leg is caught in a trap, and a chimpanzee confined to a small cage and injected with various drugs is likely to suffer considerably. Anti-speciesists believe that consideration of others' interests shouldn't depend on the abilities an animal has, only on the fact that it has interests. The most important relevant feature of an animal with interests is its capacity to suffer – that is a precondition of having interests at all. Given that we know that non-human animals do have an interest in not suffering, for Singer and many other anti-speciesists it follows that we should be vegetarians (possibly vegans), and that we should refrain from most or possibly all animal experimentation. The test should be whether we are prepared to carry out precisely the same sort of experiment on a child who is of a similar mental capability to the animal in question. Besides that, precisely the sorts of arguments that speciesists use for treating non-human animals as inferior to humans and less deserving of respect could be used by highly intelligent aliens as justification for rearing human beings as food.

CRITICISM OF ANTI-SPECIESISM

CHIMPANZEE OR HUMAN?

Imagine that a chimpanzee and a young child with exactly equal mental capability are trapped in a burning building and you are only able to save one of them. If you chose to save the chimpanzee rather than the child, would you have done something wrong? Many people believe that hypothetical thought experiments such as this show that at the very least many people have very strong intuitions that we ought to have more concern for members of our own species than for those of another species. What about if the child has brain damage, and the chimpanzee has greater mental capabilities than the child?

Many people would maintain that even in these circumstances it would be wrong to save the chimpanzee before the child. Indeed, where there is a choice between species it always seems right, intuitively, to prefer the human, even if that individual human has more restricted mental capabilities than the animal. Anti-speciesists claim that these intuitions are to some degree misguided, that the chimpanzee's interests in continued existence need to be given adequate consideration, and that if someone is prepared to kill a chimpanzee in such circumstances, they should be absolutely clear why they would not treat a child with equal or inferior mental capacities in precisely the same way.

DO ANIMALS HAVE RIGHTS?

Some thinkers have gone further than saying that animals have interests in continued existence and a good level of welfare; they have argued that animals have moral rights that we should respect, such as the right not to be harmed, and that these should be recognized (where they are not already) in law. Indeed, some commentators refer to those who have concerns over animal welfare as being part of the 'animal rights' movement.

CRITICISM OF ANIMAL RIGHTS

RIGHTS IMPLY DUTIES

Against this, many philosophers have argued that it is a mistake to attribute rights to any non-human animals. This is because rights imply duties. You can't have moral rights unless you are capable of taking on responsibilities that go with the rights. But non-human animals can't have any duties. They can't understand any notion of rights, because they lack the capacity to understand language. Rights only make sense in a human world in which we can acknowledge and meet our duties to others. In order to enter the realm of rights you have to be capable of being a member of a moral community, and be able to act morally yourself. Notice that even if you accept this argument, it doesn't follow that you can treat animals in any way you wish. Many of those who argue for greater concern for animals' interests completely reject the notion that animals have moral rights, but they do argue that animal suffering and animal welfare should concern us greatly, or that treating animals badly is a form of indirect harm to human beings.

Against this attack on the notion of animals having moral rights, it could be argued that some human beings incapable of having duties nevertheless have rights. For example, someone in a persistent vegetative state still has rights, and many people argue that unborn children in the later stages of pregnancy also have rights; many more believe that children who have not yet learnt to talk have rights. This is so, even if, tragically, the children in question stand no chance of developing intellectually to a level where they can understand and undertake any sort of moral duty (when, for example, they have very severe brain damage). If such human beings have rights, even though they are incapable of taking on duties, then surely it is possible for animals to have rights too.

INDIRECT DUTIES TO ANIMALS

A different approach to the question of how we should treat animals is based on the idea that we don't have any direct duties towards them at all, and needn't have a concern for their interests. Our apparent duties towards animals are really *indirect* duties towards other people. What this means is that although it is still wrong to harm animals in many circumstances, the wrongness lies in our duties to ourselves and to other people, not in any duties that we have towards animals. For these thinkers the ability to reason, to be capable of responsible action, and so on, are prerequisites of having rights. Animals are not sufficiently developed psychologically and morally to merit the possession of rights.

For Immanuel Kant, for example, the reason why harming animals is wrong has nothing to do with the pain the animals feel. It is because of the damage that it does to our character and its tendency to undermine a disposition that leads to good relations with other human beings that it is wrong. The suggestion is that someone who, for example, cruelly beats their dog will be more likely to be cruel to human beings as a result. We should, rightly, despise cruelty on this view, but not because of any intrinsic evil in cruelty, but rather because someone capable of cruelty to non-human animals is likely to be capable of cruelty to human beings too. Cruelty to animals damages human beings' moral characters. The dog's pain, for Kant, is not directly relevant to the assessment of the action. So our duty not to harm the dog isn't a duty towards the dog itself, but rather to other human beings.

CRITICISM OF INDIRECT DUTY VIEW

IMPLAUSIBILITY

For a utilitarian, such as Jeremy Bentham, it was obvious that the pain felt by animals was relevant to moral action. It had to be treated seriously. For anyone who has seen an animal in extreme pain it seems implausible to think that all that is morally bad about causing such pain is the effect of the action on the perpetrator. We can recognize that the corrupting effects on the individual human being are bad too, but for many people it is an unshakeable intuition that the animal's experience of pain is irrelevant to the case.

RESTS ON AN UNPROVEN EMPIRICAL CLAIM

Behind the indirect duty view lies an empirical claim, namely that all cruelty perpetrated on animals brutalizes human beings towards other human beings. But this view may not be accurate. If it isn't, then Kant's approach would be hard to justify. If cruelty to animals only sometimes has this effect, then it would not follow that we always have a duty to be humane towards animals. For example, if empirical research showed that traditional veal farming, which involves keeping calves away from daylight, confined in small crates without straw, did not have a corrupting effect on veal farmers' interactions with human beings, despite its being cruel towards non-human animals, then there would be no indirect argument against the cruelty of veal farming.

CONCLUSION

Some critics of philosophy claim that it is a pointless activity that leaves everything exactly as it is. The philosophical examination of animal welfare is an area in which ideas have had a significant impact on society and in many countries have led to changes to the law.

The next chapter focuses on political philosophy, another area in which philosophy has changed how people think and act.

FURTHER READING

Rosalind Hursthouse's *Humans and Other Animals: An Introduction with Readings* (London: Routledge, 2000), originally written as part of an Open University philosophy course, gives a very clear critical overview of many of the topics covered in this chapter, and provides appropriate readings from major thinkers in the area. Hursthouse also explores how virtue theory can illuminate questions about our treatment of other animals.

The Animal Ethics Anthology (2nd edition, London: Routledge, 2008), edited by Susan Armstrong and Richard G. Botzler, is a wide-ranging anthology on animal ethics and animal minds.

Peter Singer's *Practical Ethics* (3rd edition, Cambridge: Cambridge University Press, 2011) includes a discussion of speciesism.

Roger Scruton's *Animal Rights and Wrongs* (revised edition, London: Continuum, 2006) is critical of the idea that animals have rights.

4

POLITICS

What is equality? What is freedom? Are these worthwhile goals? How can they be achieved? What justification can be given for the state restricting the freedom of law-breakers? Are there any circumstances in which you should break the law? These are important questions for anyone. Political philosophers have attempted to clarify and answer them. Political philosophy is an immense subject, overlapping with ethics, economics, political science, and the history of ideas. Political philosophers usually write in response to the political situations in which they find themselves. In this area more than most, knowledge of the historical background is important for understanding a philosopher's arguments. Clearly there is no room for historical stage-setting in this short book. For those interested in the history of ideas the further reading at the end of the chapter should be useful.

In this chapter I focus on the central political concepts of equality, democracy, freedom, punishment, and civil disobedience, examining the philosophical questions to which they give rise.

EQUALITY

Equality is often presented as a political goal, an ideal worth aiming at. Those who argue for some form of equality are known as egalitarians. The motivation for achieving this equality is usually a moral one: it may be grounded on the Christian belief that we are all equal in the eyes of God, a Kantian belief in the rationality of equality of respect for all persons, or perhaps a utilitarian belief that treating people equally is the best way to maximize happiness. Egalitarians argue that governments should be striving to make the move from recognizing moral equality to providing some kind of equality in the lives of those they govern.

But how are we to understand 'equality'? Obviously human beings could never be equal in every respect. Individuals differ in intelligence, beauty, athletic prowess, height, hair colour, place of birth, dress sense, and many other ways. It would be ridiculous to argue that people should be absolutely equal in every respect. Complete uniformity has little appeal. Egalitarians can't be proposing a world populated by clones. Yet, despite the obvious absurdity of interpreting equality as complete uniformity, some opponents of egalitarianism persist in portraying it in this way. This is an example of setting up a straw man: creating an easy target simply to knock it down. They think that they have refuted egalitarianism by pointing out the important ways in which people differ, or by making the point that even if near uniformity could be achieved, people would very quickly revert to something like their previous condition. However, such an attack is only successful against a caricature of the theory and leaves most versions of egalitarianism unscathed.

Equality is, then, always equality in certain respects, not in every respect. So when someone declares him- or herself to be an egalitarian it is important to discover in what sense they mean this. In other words, 'equality' used in the political context is more or less meaningless unless there is some explanation of what it is that should be more equally shared and by whom. Some of the things which egalitarians often argue should be equally or more equally distributed are money, access to employment, and political power. Even though people's tastes differ considerably, all of these things can contribute significantly to a worthwhile and enjoyable life. Distributing these goods more equally is a way of according all human beings an equality of respect.

EQUAL DISTRIBUTION OF MONEY

An extreme egalitarian might argue that money should be equally distributed between all adult human beings, everyone receiving precisely the same income. In most societies money is necessary for people to live; without it they cannot get food, shelter, or clothing. Redistribution might be justified, for instance, on utilitarian grounds as the most likely way of maximizing happiness and minimizing suffering.

CRITICISMS OF EQUAL DISTRIBUTION OF MONEY

IMPRACTICAL AND SHORT-LIVED

It is fairly obvious that equal distribution of money is an unattainable goal. The practical difficulties of equal distribution of money within one city would be immense; to distribute money equally amongst every adult human being would be a logistical nightmare. So, realistically, the best that this sort of egalitarian could hope for would be a more equal distribution of money, perhaps through fixing a set wage given to all adults.

But even if we could get very close to an equal distribution of wealth, it would be short-lived. Different people would use their money in different ways; the clever, the deceitful, and the strong would quickly acquire the wealth of the weak, the foolish, and the ignorant. Some people would squander their money; others would save it. Some might gamble theirs away as soon as they got it; others might steal to increase their share. The only way of maintaining anything like an equal distribution of wealth would be by forceful intervention from on high. This would no doubt involve unpleasant intrusion into people's lives, and would limit their freedom to do what they want to do.

DIFFERENT PEOPLE DESERVE DIFFERENT AMOUNTS

Another objection to any attempt to achieve an equal distribution of money is that different people deserve different financial rewards for the jobs that they do, and the contribution that they make to society. So, for example, it is sometimes claimed that rich heads of industry deserve the vast salaries which they pay themselves because of their relatively greater contribution to the nation: they make it possible for other people to work and increase the general economic well-being of the whole country in which they operate.

Even if they don't *deserve* the higher wages, perhaps higher wages are needed as an incentive for getting the job done efficiently, the overall benefits to society outweighing the costs: without them there might be much less to go round for everyone. Without the incentive of high pay, no one capable of doing the job would take it on.

Here we encounter a fundamental difference between egalitarians and those who believe that gross inequalities in wealth between individuals are acceptable. It is a basic belief of most egalitarians that only moderate differences in wealth between individuals are acceptable, and that ideally those differences should correspond to differences in need. This suggests a further criticism of the principle of equal distribution of money.

DIFFERENT PEOPLE HAVE DIFFERENT NEEDS

Some people need more money to live than others. Someone who can only survive if given daily expensive medical care would be very unlikely to live very long in a society in which each individual is restricted to an equal share of the total wealth of that society, unless of course the society was a particularly rich one. A method of distribution based on individual need would go further towards the goal of respect for common humanity than would one of equal distribution of money.

NO RIGHT TO REDISTRIBUTE

Some philosophers argue that no matter how attractive a goal redistribution of money might seem, it would violate the rights of individuals to hold on to their property, and that that violation is always morally wrong. These philosophers claim that rights always trump any other considerations, such as utilitarian ones. Robert Nozick (1938–2002), in his *Anarchy, State and Utopia*, takes this position, emphasizing a basic right to keep property that has been legally acquired.

Such philosophers are left with the problem of saying precisely what these rights are and where they come from. By 'rights' they do not mean legal rights, though such rights may coincide with legal rights in a just society: legal rights are those laid down by government or the appropriate authority. The rights in question are natural rights, which should ideally guide the formation of laws. Some philosophers have taken issue with the idea that there could be such natural rights: Bentham famously dismissed the notion as 'nonsense on stilts'. At the very least a defender of the view that the state has no right to redistribute wealth should be able to explain the source of the supposed natural property rights, rather than simply assert their existence. Advocates of natural rights have conspicuously failed to do this.

EQUAL OPPORTUNITY IN EMPLOYMENT

Many egalitarians believe that everyone should have equal opportunities even if there can be no equality of distribution of wealth. One important area in which there is a great deal of inequality of treatment is that of employment. Equality of opportunity in employment does not mean that everyone should be allowed to do whatever job they want to do, regardless of their ability: the idea that anyone who wants to become a dentist or a surgeon should be allowed to do so, no matter how bad their eye/hand co-ordination, is clearly absurd. What equality of opportunity means is equal opportunity for all those with relevant skills and abilities to do the job in question. This could still be seen as a form of unequal treatment, since some people are lucky enough to be born with greater genetic potential than others, or have received a better education, and so have a head start in an apparently equal contest in the job market. However, equality of opportunity in employment is usually advocated as just one aspect of a move towards greater equality of various kinds, such as equality of access to education.

The demand for equality of opportunity in employment is largely motivated by widespread racial and sexual discrimination in some professions. Egalitarians argue that anyone with relevant qualifications should be given equal consideration when seeking employment. No one should be discriminated against on racial or sexual grounds, except in those very rare cases where race or sex can be considered a relevant qualification for doing the job in question: for instance, it would be impossible for a woman to be a sperm donor, so it would not transgress any principle of equality of opportunity to rule out any female applicants for the role.

Some egalitarians go even further than demanding equality of treatment when applying for jobs: they argue that it is important to get rid of existing imbalances in particular professions, for instance the predominance of male over female judges. Their method of redressing existing imbalances is known as reverse discrimination.

REVERSE DISCRIMINATION

Reverse discrimination means actively recruiting people from previously underprivileged groups. In other words, reverse discriminators deliberately treat job applicants unequally in that they are biased towards people from groups against which discrimination has usually been directed. The point of treating people unequally in this way is that it is intended to speed up the process of society becoming more equal, not only by getting rid of existing imbalances within certain professions, but also by providing role models for young people from the traditionally less privileged groups to imitate and look up to.

So, for instance, there are more male university philosophy lecturers than female in Britain, despite the fact that many women study the subject as undergraduates. An advocate of reverse discrimination would argue that, rather than waiting for this situation to change gradually, we should act positively, and discriminate in favour of women applicants for university lectureships. This means that if a man and a woman both applied for the same post and were of roughly equal ability, we should choose the woman. But most defenders of reverse discrimination would go further than this, and argue that even if the woman were a weaker candidate than the man, provided she was competent to perform the duties associated with the job, we should employ her in preference to him. Reverse discrimination is only a temporary measure used until the percentage of members of the traditionally excluded group roughly reflects the percentage of members of this group in the population as a whole. In some countries it is illegal; in others it is required by law.

CRITICISMS OF REVERSE DISCRIMINATION

ANTI-EGALITARIAN

The aims of reverse discrimination may be egalitarian, but some people feel that the way it achieves them is unfair. For a staunch egalitarian, a principle of equality of opportunity in employment means that any form of discrimination on non-relevant grounds must be avoided. The only grounds for treating applicants differently is that they have relevantly different attributes. Yet the whole justification of reverse discrimination rests on the assumption that in most jobs such things as the sex, sexual preferences, or racial origin of the applicant are not relevant. So no matter how attractive the end result of reverse discrimination may be, it should be unacceptable to someone committed to equality of opportunity as a fundamental principle.

A supporter of reverse discrimination might reply that the current state of affairs is much more unfair to members of disadvantaged groups than a situation in which reverse discrimination is widely practised. Alternatively, in cases where such an extreme policy is appropriate, the racial origins or sex of the applicant can actually become relevant qualifications for doing the job, since part of the job of anyone selected in this way would be to act as a role model to show that the job could be done by members of this group. However, it is debatable whether this latter situation is one of reverse discrimination at all: if these attributes are relevant ones, then taking them into account when selecting personnel is not really a form of discrimination but rather an adjustment of what we take to be the most important qualities needed for doing a particular job.

MAY LEAD TO RESENTMENT

Although the aim of reverse discrimination is to create a society in which access to certain professions is more equally distributed, in practice it may be the cause of further discrimination against disadvantaged groups. Those who fail to get a particular job because they happen not to come from a disadvantaged group may feel resentment against those who get jobs largely because of their sex or racial origin. This is a particular problem when employers take on candidates who are visibly incapable of carrying out their duties well. Not only does this confirm the worst prejudices of their employers and colleagues, but also results in them being poor role models for other members of their group. In the long term this may undermine the general move towards equality of access to jobs that reverse discrimination is supposed to achieve. However, this criticism can be met by making sure that the minimum standard of ability of a candidate who gets a job because of reverse discrimination is relatively high.

POLITICAL EQUALITY: DEMOCRACY

Another area in which equality is pursued is that of political participation. Democracy is often celebrated as a method of giving all citizens a share in political decision-making. However, the word 'democracy' is used in a number of different ways. Two potentially conflicting views of democracy stand out. The first emphasizes the need for members of the population to have an opportunity to participate in the government of the state, usually through voting. The second emphasizes the need for a democratic state to reflect the true interests of the people, even though the people may themselves be ignorant of where their true interests lie. Here I shall concentrate on the first type of democracy.

In Ancient Greece a democracy was a city-state ruled by the people rather than by the few (an oligarchy), or by one person (a monarchy). Ancient Athens is usually considered a model of democracy, though it would be wrong to think of it as run by the people as a whole, since women, slaves, and many other non-citizens who dwelt in the city-state were not allowed to participate. No democratic state allows *all* those who live within its control to vote: that would include numerous people who would be incapable of understanding what they were doing, such as young children and the severely mentally ill. However, a state which denied a large proportion of its people political participation would not today merit the name democracy.

DIRECT DEMOCRACY

Early democratic states were direct democracies; that is, those who were eligible to vote discussed and voted on each issue rather than electing representatives. Direct democracies are only feasible with a small number of participants or when relatively few decisions have to be made. The practical difficulties of a large number of people voting on a wide variety of issues are immense, though it is possible that electronic communication will eventually permit this. But even if this were achieved, for such a democracy to arrive at reasonable decisions, voters would have to have a good grasp of the issues on which they were voting, something which would require time and a programme of education. It would probably be expecting too much for all citizens to keep abreast of the relevant issues. Today's democracies are representative democracies.

REPRESENTATIVE DEMOCRACY

In a representative democracy elections are held in which voters select their favoured representatives. These representatives then take part in the day-to-day decision-making process, which may itself be organized on some sort of democratic principles. There are several different ways in which such elections are conducted: some demand a majority decision; others, such as the one used in Britain, operate a first-past-the-post system which allows representatives to be elected even if a majority of the electorate do not vote for them, provided that no one else receives more votes than they do.

Representative democracies achieve government by the people in some ways but not in others. They achieve government by the people in so far as those elected have been chosen by the people. Once elected, however, the representatives are not usually bound on particular issues by the wishes of the people. Having frequent elections is a safeguard against abuse of office: those representatives who do not respect the wishes of the electorate are unlikely to be re-elected.

CRITICISMS OF DEMOCRACY

AN ILLUSION

Some theorists, particularly those influenced by Karl Marx (1818–83), have attacked the forms of democracy sketched above as providing a merely illusory sense of participation in political decision-making. They claim that voting procedures won't guarantee rule by the people. Some voters may not understand where their best interests lie, or may be duped by skilful speech-makers. And besides, the range of candidates offered in most elections doesn't offer voters a genuine choice. It is hard to see why this sort of democracy is so praised when it typically amounts to choosing between two or three candidates with virtually indistinguishable political policies. This, say the Marxists, is mere 'bourgeois democracy', which simply reflects existing power relations, which are themselves the result of economic relations. Until these power relations have been redressed, giving the population a chance to vote in elections is a waste of time.

VOTERS AREN'T EXPERTS

Other critics of democracy, most notably Plato, have pointed out that sound political decision-making requires a great deal of expertise, expertise which many voters do not have. Thus direct democracy would very likely result in a very poor political system, since the state would be in the hands of people who had little skill or knowledge of what they were doing. The captain, not the passengers, should steer the ship.

A similar argument can be used to attack representative democracy. Many voters aren't in a position to assess the suitability of a particular candidate. Since they aren't in a position to assess political policy, they choose their representatives on the basis of non-relevant attributes such as how good-looking they are, or whether they have a nice smile. Or else their voting is determined by unexamined prejudices about political parties. As a result, many excellent potential representatives remain unelected, and many unsuitable ones get chosen on the basis of inappropriate qualities they happen to have.

However, this evidence could be turned around and used as an argument for educating citizens for participation in democracy, rather than abandoning democracy altogether. And even if this is not possible, it may still be true that representative democracy is, of all available alternatives, the most likely to promote the interests of the people.

THE PARADOX OF DEMOCRACY

I believe that capital punishment is barbaric and should never occur in a civilized state. If in a referendum on the topic I vote against instating capital punishment, and yet the majority decision is that it should be instated, I am faced with a paradox. As someone committed to democratic principles I believe that the majority decision should be enacted. As an individual with strongly held beliefs about the wrongness of capital punishment I believe that capital punishment should never be permitted. So it seems that in this case I both believe that capital punishment should occur (as the result of the majority decision) *and* that it shouldn't occur (because of my personal beliefs). But these two beliefs are incompatible. Anyone committed to democratic principles is likely to be faced with a similar paradox when they find themselves in a minority.

This does not completely undermine the notion of democracy, but it does draw attention to the possibility of conflicts of conscience and majority decision, something which I discuss below in the section on civil disobedience. Anyone committed to democratic principles will have to decide the relative weight given to individual beliefs and collective decisions. They will also have to spell out what 'commitment to democratic principles' means.

FREEDOM

Like 'democracy', 'freedom' is a word which has been used in many different ways. There are two main senses of freedom in the political context: the negative and the positive. These were identified and analysed by Isaiah Berlin (1909–97) in a famous article, 'Two Concepts of Liberty'.

NEGATIVE FREEDOM

One definition of freedom is the absence of coercion. Coercion is when other people force you to behave in a particular way, or force you to stop behaving in a particular way. If no one is coercing you then you are free in this negative sense of freedom.

If someone has put you in prison and is holding you there, then you are not free. Nor are you free if you want to leave the country but have had your passport confiscated; nor if you want to live openly in a homosexual relationship but will be prosecuted if you do so. Negative freedom is freedom from obstacle or restraint. If no one is actively preventing you from doing something, then in that respect you are free.

Most governments restrict the freedom of individuals to some extent. Their justification for doing so is usually the need to protect all members of society. If everyone were completely at liberty to do whatever they wanted to do, then the strongest and most ruthless would probably thrive at the expense of the weak. However, many liberal political philosophers believe that there ought to be an area of individual liberty which is sacrosanct, which, provided that you are not harming anyone else, is not the government's business. In his *On Liberty*, for instance, John Stuart Mill argued forcefully that individuals should be allowed to conduct their own 'experiments of living' free from state interference, just so long as nobody was harmed in the process.

CRITICISMS OF NEGATIVE FREEDOM

WHAT COUNTS AS HARM?

In practice it may be difficult to decide what is to count as harm to other people. Does it, for instance, include harming others' feelings? If it does, then all sorts of 'experiments of living' will have to be ruled out since they offend a great number of people. For instance, a prudish neighbour may be offended by the knowledge that a naturist couple next door never wear clothes. Or, for that matter, the naturist couple may be offended by the knowledge that so many people do wear clothes. Both the naturists and their neighbours may feel harmed by other people's lifestyles. Mill did not believe that taking offence should count as a serious harm, but drawing the line between being offended and being harmed is not always easy; for instance, many people would consider blasphemy against their religion far more harmful to them than physical injury. On what grounds can we say that they are wrong?

POSITIVE FREEDOM

Some philosophers have attacked the idea that negative freedom is the sort of freedom we should strive to increase. They argue that positive freedom is a far more important political goal. Positive freedom is freedom to exercise control over your own life. You are free in the positive sense if you actually exercise control, and not free if you don't, even if you are not actually constrained in any way. Most defenders of the positive concept of freedom believe that true freedom lies in some kind of self-realization through individuals, or indeed states, making their own life choices.

For instance, if someone is an alcoholic and is driven against their better judgement to spend all their money on wild drinking sprees, then does this amount to exercising freedom? It seems intuitively implausible, particularly if in sober moments the alcoholic regrets these binges. Rather we would tend to think of the alcoholic as controlled by drink: a slave to impulse. Despite the lack of constraint, on the positive account the alcoholic is not genuinely free.

Even an advocate of negative freedom might argue that alcoholics, like children, should be coerced in some ways, on the ground that they are not fully responsible for their actions. But if someone consistently makes foolish life decisions, squanders all their talents, and so on, then according to Mill's principles we are entitled to reason with them, but never to coerce them into a better way of life. That would be a form of unjustified paternalism, that is, acting as a controlling parent towards someone who has reached an age when they should be free to make their own choices and their own mistakes. For Mill it is not acceptable to intervene in another adult's life for their 'own good' unless they are harming someone else, or are mentally incapable of acting for themselves. Coercion would involve limiting their negative freedom. Those who defend a principle of positive freedom might argue that such a person is not truly free until they realize their potential and overcome their wayward tendencies. It is a short step from this to arguing in favour of coercion as a path to genuine freedom.

Isaiah Berlin maintains that the positive conception of freedom can be used to license all sorts of unjust coercion: agents of the state may justify forcing you to behave in certain ways, on the grounds that they are helping to increase your freedom. Indeed, he points out that historically the positive concept of freedom has frequently been abused in this way. It is not that there is anything intrinsically wrong with the positive conception; rather it is simply that history has shown it to be a dangerous weapon when misused.

FREEDOM OF SPEECH

A mark of a totalitarian regime is the absence of free expression. Most Western societies pride themselves on the freedom of their citizens to express a wide range of views and contribute to public debates without fear of censorship. Yet freedom of expression in this context is never total freedom. There are always legal limits on what you can publish or speak with impunity, whether these are laws against pornography, libel, or, in some cases, blasphemy.

Mill set out a strong case for tolerating free speech in most contexts. The limits of free speech should be where the expressed view caused harm rather than merely offence to other people. If you abuse free speech and incite violence, then you should be censored. But, Mill argued, you should be free to express your views up to the point where you run the risk of harming other people: offending them is acceptable. He used a range of arguments to defend freedom from censorship. Here I will just sketch two of these.

First, Mill thought any censor must assume infallibility. That is, the censor assumes that he or she can never be wrong. But this is an absurd assumption for a censor since we all make mistakes. Mill takes it for granted that the main motivation for censorship is the belief that the censored idea is false. So on this view the censor runs the risk of preventing some true and potentially important ideas from getting a wider hearing.

Second, Mill argued that unless views are regularly challenged they are likely to be held as dead dogmas. Even if the view expressed is false, the very fact of the orthodox view being challenged forces its holders to clarify and defend their beliefs. The result is that we end up holding beliefs because we understand the arguments in support of them, not just because we are told that they are true. For example, those who believe that Darwinian evolution is by far the best explanation of animals' adaptation to their environments (which it is) may believe that creationists who deny evolution are just wrong. On Mill's view, evolutionists should tolerate public criticism of their views by creationists because this will force them to give the reasons for their belief that evolution is the best explanation, and help them to hold this as a living belief. Through the collision between truth and falsehood, the truth will emerge victorious and with a greater power to influence action. And besides, the process of having our beliefs challenged can lead us to modify them for the better, since many challenges contain an element of truth in them, even if they are not as powerful as their proponents believe.

CRITICISMS OF MILL ON FREE SPEECH

NOT ALWAYS A QUESTION OF TRUTH

Mill's focus was on censorship of views that might be true or false. He was writing in the nineteenth century. In the twenty-first century, the usual argument for censorship is that the suppressed material is dangerous, not that it is false. For instance, if someone puts information on the Internet about how to make a lethal bomb from readily available chemicals, then the reason for suppressing such information would be that it is true and dangerous, not that it is false.

Mill could have responded to such objections by pointing out that his defence of free speech allowed for censorship when there was a serious risk of other people being harmed by the views expressed.

A RIGHT TO FREE SPEECH?

Mill's arguments for free speech turn on the *consequences* of censorship. The risk here is that in cases where there would be clear benefits resulting from censorship, the consequentialist will be obliged to accept that censorship is legitimate. In other words, Mill's arguments don't give individuals anything like a right to free speech. What they purport to show is that there are extremely beneficial consequences to society that ensue from tolerating free speech, even when the views being expressed are false.

A stronger line of argument would be to claim that we all have a right, a human right, to free speech, that it is part of a state's recognition of an individual citizen's humanity that it allows that citizen to express whatever views he or she cares to publish. On this account it is always a denial of someone's basic human right if you silence them. The trouble with this, though, is that it isn't obvious where human rights come from. So the defence of freedom of speech on the grounds that it is a basic human right needs some underpinning. It is true that freedom of expression is listed as Article 19 of the 1948 Universal Declaration of Human Rights. But, the philosophical question remains, on what is that right grounded?

REMOVING FREEDOM: PUNISHMENT

What can justify taking freedom away as a form of punishment? In other words, what reasons can be given for restraining people, removing liberty in the negative sense? As we have seen in the previous section, the notion of positive freedom can be used to justify coercing individuals in some ways: only by being protected against themselves can such people achieve true freedom.

Philosophers have attempted to justify state punishment of individuals in four main ways: as retribution, as deterrent, as protection for society, and as reform of the person punished. The first is usually defended from a deontological position; the other three typically on consequentialist grounds.

PUNISHMENT AS RETRIBUTION

In its simplest form, retributivism is the view that those who intentionally break the law deserve the punishment they get, regardless of whether there are any beneficial consequences for the individuals concerned or for society. Those who intentionally break the law deserve to suffer. Clearly there will be many people who are incapable of full responsibility for their law-breaking, and these deserve milder punishment, or in extreme cases, such as the severely mentally ill, treatment. However, in general, according to a retributivist theory, punishment is justified as the appropriate response to wrongdoing. Moreover, the severity of the punishment should reflect the severity of the crime. In its simplest form of 'an eye for an eye' (sometimes known as *lex talionis*), retributivism demands an exactly proportional response to the crime committed. For some crimes such as blackmail it is difficult to see what this response could amount to: presumably the judge wouldn't be expected to sentence the blackmailer to six months' blackmail. Similarly it is hard to understand how a poverty-stricken thief who steals a gold watch could be punished in exact proportion to the crime. This is only a problem for the principle of an eye for an eye; with more sophisticated forms of retributivism the punishment need not mirror the crime.

CRITICISMS OF RETRIBUTIVISM

IT APPEALS TO BASER FEELINGS

Retributivism gets much of its force from feelings of revenge. Getting one's own back is a very basic human response to being harmed. Opponents of retributivism recognize how widespread this feeling is but argue that state punishment should be founded on a sounder principle than 'tit for tat'. However, those who defend hybrid justifications of punishment often include it as an element in their theory.

IT IGNORES EFFECTS

The main criticism of retributivism is that it pays no attention to the effects of the punishment on the criminal or on society. Questions of deterrence, reform, and protection are irrelevant. According to retributivists, criminals deserve to be punished whether this has a beneficial effect on them or not. Consequentialists object to this on the grounds that no action can be morally right unless it has beneficial consequences, to which deontologists might reply that, if an action is morally justified, it is so whatever the consequences.

DETERRENCE

A common justification of punishment is that it discourages law-breaking: both by the individual who is punished, and by others who are aware that the punishment has taken place and will be meted out to them if they break the law. If you know that you are likely to end up in prison, so the argument goes, you will be less likely to choose a career as a burglar than you would if you thought you could get away without punishment. This justifies punishing even those who will not be reformed by the punishment: it is more important that punishment is seen to be the result of crime than that the individual concerned is changed. This sort of justification focuses exclusively on the consequences of punishment. The suffering of those who lose their liberty is outweighed by the benefits to society.

CRITICISMS OF DETERRENCE

PUNISHING THE INNOCENT

A very serious criticism of the deterrent theory of punishment is that, at least in its simplest form, it could be used to justify punishing people who are innocent of any crime, or of the crime for which they are punished. In some situations punishing a scapegoat who is widely believed to have committed a particular crime will have a very strong deterrent effect on others who had been contemplating similar crimes, particularly if the general public remains unaware that the victim of the punishment is in fact innocent. In such cases, it seems that we would be justified in punishing an innocent person – an unattractive consequence of this theory. Any plausible deterrent theory of punishment will have to meet this objection.

IT DOESN'T WORK

Some critics of punishment as deterrence argue that it simply doesn't work. Even extreme punishments, such as the death penalty, don't deter serial killers; milder punishments, such as fines and short periods of imprisonment, don't deter thieves.

This sort of criticism relies on empirical data. The relation between types of punishment and crime rates is extremely difficult to work out, as there are so many factors which can distort the interpretation of the data. However, if it could be shown conclusively that punishment had little or no deterrent effect, this would be a devastating blow for this particular justification of punishment.

PROTECTION OF SOCIETY

Another justification of punishment based on its alleged beneficial consequences emphasizes the need to protect society from people who have a tendency to break the law. If someone has broken into one house, then they may well break into another house. So the state is justified in locking them away in order to prevent them reoffending. This justification is most often used in the case of violent crimes such as rape or murder.

CRITICISMS OF PROTECTION OF SOCIETY

ONLY RELEVANT FOR SOME CRIMES

Some types of crime, such as rape, may be committed again and again by the same person. In such cases restricting the liberty of the criminal will minimize the chance of the crime being committed again. However, other crimes are one-off. For instance, a wife with a lifetime's resentment of her husband may finally get up the courage to poison his muesli. This woman may pose no threat whatsoever to anyone else. She committed a very serious crime, but this is not one that she would ever be likely to recommit. For such a woman, protection of society would not provide a justification for punishing her. However, in practice there is no easy way to identify those criminals who will not reoffend.

IT DOESN'T WORK

Another criticism of this justification of punishment is that imprisoning criminals only protects society in the short term and that in the long term it actually results in a more dangerous society, because while in prison criminals teach each other how to get away with crime. So, unless life imprisonment is given for every serious crime, imprisonment is unlikely to protect society.

Again, this is an empirical argument. If its claims are true, then there are good grounds for combining protection of society with some attempt to reform the habits of criminals.

REFORM

A further justification of punishing those who break the law is the punishment's tendency to reform the wrongdoers. That is, punishment serves to change their characters so that they will no longer commit crimes when released. On this view removing freedom can serve as a form of treatment.

CRITICISMS OF REFORM

ONLY RELEVANT FOR SOME CRIMINALS

Some criminals are not in need of reform. Those who commit one-off crimes should not be punished according to this justification, since they are unlikely to break the law again. Also some criminals are clearly beyond reform: there would be no point in punishing these either, assuming they could be identified. This in itself is not a criticism of the theory, just a more detailed look at what the theory implies. However, many people will find these implications unacceptable.

IT DOESN'T WORK

Existing punishments rarely reform criminals. However, not all types of punishment are doomed to failure in this respect. This sort of empirical argument would only be fatal to the idea of punishment as reform if it could be shown that such attempts at reform could never be successful. Nevertheless, very few justifications focus exclusively on the reformative aspects of punishment. The most plausible justifications make reform an element of the justification along with deterrence and protection of society. Such hybrid justifications are usually based on consequentialist moral principles.

CIVIL DISOBEDIENCE

So far we have looked at justifications for punishing law-breakers. The grounds for punishing them were moral ones. But could it ever be morally acceptable to break a law? In this section I look at a particular kind of law-breaking which is justified on moral grounds: civil disobedience.

Some people argue that law-breaking can never be justified: if you are dissatisfied with the law you should try to get it changed through legal channels such as campaigning, letter-writing, and so on. But there are many cases when such legal protest is completely useless. There is a tradition of breaking the law in such circumstances known as civil disobedience. The occasion for civil disobedience arises when people find that they are being asked to obey laws or government policies which they consider to be unjust.

Civil disobedience has brought about important changes in law and government policy. A famous example is the suffragette movement in Britain, which managed to publicize its aim of getting votes for women through a campaign of public civil disobedience which included protesters chaining themselves to railings. Limited emancipation was finally achieved in 1918, when women over the age of thirty were permitted to vote in elections, and was partly due to the social impact of the First World War. Nevertheless, the suffragette movement had a significant role to play in changing the unjust law which prevented women from participating in supposedly democratic elections.

Mahatma Gandhi and Martin Luther King Jr were both passionate advocates of civil disobedience. Gandhi was hugely influential in promoting Indian independence by means of non-violent illegal protest, which eventually led to the withdrawal of the British Raj; Martin Luther King Jr's defiance of racial prejudice by similar methods helped to guarantee basic civil rights for black Americans in the southern states of the USA.

Another example of civil disobedience is provided by some Americans' refusal to fight in the Vietnam War, despite being called up by their government. Some did this on the grounds that they believed any killing to be morally wrong, and so thought it more important to break the law than to fight and possibly kill other human beings. Others did not object to all wars but felt that the war in Vietnam was an unjust war which put civilians at immense risk for no good reason. The extent of opposition to the war in Vietnam eventually led to the United States' withdrawal. Public law-breaking undoubtedly fuelled this opposition.

The tradition of civil disobedience is one of non-violent, public law-breaking designed to bring attention to unjust laws or government policies. Those who act within this tradition of civil disobedience do not break the law simply for personal gain; they do it in order to draw attention to an unjust law or morally objectionable government policy, and to maximize publicity for their cause. This is why it usually takes place in public, preferably in the presence of journalists, photographers, and television cameras. For instance, an American conscript who threw away his draft card during the Vietnam War, and then hid from the army simply because he was scared of fighting and didn't want to die, would not be performing an act of civil disobedience. It would be an act of self-preservation. If he acted in the same way, not from fear for his personal safety, but on moral grounds, yet did this secretly, not making his case public in any way, then it still would not qualify as an act of civil disobedience. In contrast, another conscript who burnt his draft card in public, while being filmed for television and making a statement about why he thought American involvement in Vietnam immoral, would be engaging in civil disobedience.

The aim of civil disobedience is ultimately to change particular laws or government policies, not to undermine the rule of law completely. Those who act within the tradition of civil disobedience usually avoid any kind of violence, not only because it can undermine their cause by encouraging retaliation and thus an escalation of conflict, but primarily because their justification for law-breaking is on moral grounds, and most moral principles only permit harm to other people in extreme situations, such as if you are attacked and need to defend yourself.

Terrorists, or freedom fighters (which you call them depends on how sympathetic you are to their aims), use acts of violence for political ends. Like those who engage in acts of civil disobedience, they want to change the existing state of affairs, not for private gain, but for the general good as they see it. Where they differ is in the methods they are prepared to use to bring about this change.

CRITICISMS OF CIVIL DISOBEDIENCE

UNDEMOCRATIC

Assuming that civil disobedience takes place in some kind of democracy, it can appear to be undemocratic. If a majority of democratically elected representatives vote that a particular law should be created, or a government policy put into practice, then to break the law as a protest against this seems to go against the spirit of democracy, particularly if a very small minority of citizens are involved in the act of civil disobedience. Surely the fact that everyone is likely to find some government policies disagreeable is just the price to pay for living in a democratic state. If civil disobedience by a minority is effective, then that seems to give the few power to overturn the majority view. This seems profoundly anti-democratic. Yet if civil disobedience isn't effective, there seems little point in undertaking it. So, on this view, civil disobedience is either undemocratic or else pointless.

Against this, it is important to realize that acts of civil disobedience are intended to highlight morally unacceptable government decisions or practices. For instance, the Civil Rights movement in America in the 1960s, through well-publicized demonstrations in defiance of legally enforced racial segregation, gave worldwide publicity to the unfair treatment of black Americans. Understood in this way, civil disobedience is a technique for getting the majority or their representatives to reconsider their position on a particular issue, rather than an undemocratic way of getting law or policy changed.

SLIPPERY SLOPE TO LAWLESSNESS

Another objection to civil disobedience is that it encourages law-breaking, which could in the long term undermine the power of government and the rule of law, and that this risk far outweighs any possible benefits that might arise from it. Once respect for the law is undermined, even if on moral grounds, the danger is that general lawlessness will follow.

This is a slippery slope argument, an argument which suggests that if you take one step in a particular direction, you won't be able to stop a process, which will result in an obviously unattractive result. Just as when you take one step down a slippery slope, it is almost impossible to stop until you reach the bottom, so, some people claim, if you make some minor kinds of law-breaking acceptable then there will be no stopping until no one respects the law any longer. However, this sort of argument can make the end result seem inevitable when it is not. There is no reason to believe the claim that acts of civil disobedience will undermine respect for the law; to continue the metaphor of the slippery slope, there is no reason to believe that we can't dig our heels in at a certain point and say 'Here and no further'. Indeed, some advocates of civil disobedience argue that, far from undermining the rule of law, what they do indicates deep respect for the law. If someone is prepared to be punished by the state for drawing attention to what they believe to be an unjust law, this shows that they are committed to the general position that laws should be just and that just laws should be respected. This is very different from breaking a law for personal gain.

CONCLUSION

In this chapter I have discussed a number of central topics in political philosophy. Underlying all of these topics is the question of the individual's relation to the state, and in particular the source of any authority the state has over the individual, a question addressed directly in much of the further reading recommended below.

The next chapter and the one that follows it concentrate on our knowledge and understanding of the world around us, paying particular attention to the question of what we can learn through our senses.

FURTHER READING

For those interested in the history of political philosophy, *Great Political Thinkers* by Quentin Skinner, Richard Tuck, William Thomas, and Peter Singer (Oxford: Oxford University Press, 1992) provides a good introduction to the work of Machiavelli, Hobbes, Mill, and Marx. Nigel Warburton et al.'s *Reading Political Philosophy: Machiavelli to Mill* (London. Routledge and the Open University, 2001) provides a practical guide to reading some of the most important works by these philosophers.

Jonathan Wolff's *Political Philosophy: An Introduction* (2nd edition, Oxford: Oxford University Press, 1996) is a thorough and wide-ranging introduction to this area of philosophy.

Peter Singer's *Practical Ethics* (3rd edition, Cambridge: Cambridge University Press, 2011), a book which I recommended as further reading for Chapter 2, includes a discussion of equality, including equality in employment. He also puts the case for equality for animals. Janet Radcliffe Richards's *The Sceptical Feminist* (2nd edition, London: Penguin, 1994) is a clear and incisive philosophical analysis of moral and political questions about women, including the issue of reverse discrimination in employment.

Ross Harrison's *Democracy* (London: Routledge, 1993) is a lucid introduction to one of the central concepts in political philosophy. It combines a critical survey of the history of democracy with philosophical analysis of the concept as we use it today.

Liberty, edited by David Miller (Oxford: Oxford University Press, Oxford Readings in Politics and Government, 1991), includes an abridgement of Isaiah Berlin's essay 'Two Concepts of Liberty'. John Stuart Mill's *On Liberty* (London: Penguin Classics, 1982) is the classic statement of liberalism. I discuss both Berlin and Mill in my book *Freedom: An Introduction with Readings* (London: Routledge and the Open University, 2000). I discuss free speech in my book *Free Speech: A Very Short Introduction* (Oxford: Oxford University Press, 2009).

Civil Disobedience in Focus, edited by Hugo Adam Bedau (London: Routledge, 1991), is an interesting collection of articles on the topic, including Martin Luther King Jr's 'Letter from Birmingham City Jail'.

For those wishing to study political philosophy in greater detail and at a more advanced level, Will Kymlicka's *Contemporary Political Philosophy: An Introduction* (2nd edition, Oxford: Oxford University Press, 2002) provides a critical appraisal of the main trends in current political philosophy. It is quite difficult in places.

5

APPEARANCE AND REALITY

Our basic knowledge of the external world comes through the five senses: sight, hearing, touch, smell, and taste. For most of us the sense of sight plays the key role. I know what the world out there is like because I can see it. If I am uncertain whether what I see is really there, I can usually reach out and touch it to make sure. I know that there is a fly in my soup because I can see it, and, if it comes to it, touch it and even taste it. But what is the precise relationship between what I think I see and what is actually in front of me? Can I ever be sure about what is out there? Could I be dreaming? Do objects continue to exist when nobody is observing them? Do I ever have direct experience of the external world? These are all questions about how we acquire knowledge of our surroundings; they belong to the branch of philosophy known as the theory of knowledge or epistemology.

In this chapter we will examine a number of epistemological questions, concentrating on theories of perception.

COMMON-SENSE REALISM

Common-sense realism is a view held by most people who haven't studied philosophy. It assumes that there is a world of physical objects — houses, trees, cars, goldfish, teaspoons, footballs, human bodies, philosophy books, and so on — which we can learn about directly through our five senses. These physical objects continue to exist whether or not we are perceiving them. What is more, these objects are more or less as they appear to us: goldfish really are orange, and footballs really are spherical. This is because our organs of sense perception – eyes, ears, tongue, skin, and nose – are generally reliable. They give us a realistic appreciation of what is actually out there.

However, whilst it is possible to go through life without questioning the assumptions of common-sense realism about sense perception, this view is not satisfactory. Common-sense realism does not stand up well to sceptical arguments about the reliability of the senses. Here we will examine various sceptical arguments which seem to undermine common-sense realism, before going on to examine four more sophisticated theories of perception: representative realism, idealism, phenomenalism, and causal realism.

SCEPTICISM ABOUT THE EVIDENCE OF THE SENSES

Scepticism is the view that we can never know anything for certain, that there is always some ground to doubt even our most fundamental beliefs about the world. Sceptical arguments in philosophy attempt to show that our traditional ways of finding out about the world are unreliable, and do not guarantee us knowledge of what really exists. The sceptical arguments in the following sections are based on René Descartes's arguments in the first of his *Meditations*.

THE ILLUSION ARGUMENT

The Illusion Argument is a sceptical argument which questions the reliability of the senses, and thus threatens to undermine common-sense realism. We usually trust our senses, but there are times when they mislead us. For instance, most of us have had the embarrassing experience of seeming to recognize a friend in the distance, only to discover that we are waving to a complete stranger. A straight stick, when partly immersed in water, can look bent; an apple can taste bitter if you have just been eating something very sweet; viewed from a certain angle a round coin can look oval; railway tracks seem to converge in the distance; hot weather can make the road look as if it is moving; the same dress may look crimson in subdued light and scarlet in sunlight; the moon looks larger the lower it is on the horizon. These and similar sensory illusions show that the senses are not always completely reliable: it seems unlikely that the external world really is exactly as it appears to be.

The Illusion Argument says that because our senses sometimes mislead us, we can never be certain in any particular case that they are not misleading us at that moment. This argument is a sceptical one because it challenges our everyday belief – common-sense realism – that the senses provide us with knowledge of the world.

CRITICISMS OF THE ILLUSION ARGUMENT

DEGREES OF CERTAINTY

Although I might make mistakes about seeing objects in the distance, or under unusual conditions, surely there are some observations about which I can have no reasonable doubt. For instance, I cannot seriously doubt that I am sitting at my desk writing this now, that I have a pen in my hand, and that there is a pad of paper in front of me. Similarly, I can't seriously doubt that I am in England, rather than, for instance, in Japan. There are some uncontroversial cases of knowing through which we learn the concept of knowledge. It is only because we have this background of cases of knowledge that we can doubt other beliefs: without these uncontroversial cases we would have no concept of knowledge at all, and nothing with which to contrast more doubtful beliefs.

Against this view a sceptic would point out that I could very well be wrong about what seem to be instances of certain knowledge: in dreams I may have thought that I was awake writing when in fact I was lying asleep in bed. So how can I tell that I am not dreaming that I am writing? How can I tell that I'm not lying asleep somewhere in Tokyo dreaming that I am awake in England? I have certainly dreamt stranger dreams than that. Is there anything about the experience of dreaming which can conclusively distinguish it from that of waking?

COULD I BE DREAMING?

CAN'T ALWAYS BE DREAMING

It would not make sense to say that my whole life is a dream. If I were dreaming all the time, then I would have no concept of a dream: I would have nothing with which to contrast dreaming since I would have no concept of being awake. We can only make sense of the idea of a forged banknote when genuine banknotes exist with which to compare it; similarly the idea of a dream only makes sense when we can compare it to waking life.

This is true, but it does not destroy the sceptic's position. What the sceptic is arguing is not that we might be dreaming all the time, but rather that at any one moment we cannot know for certain whether or not we are actually dreaming.

DREAMS ARE DIFFERENT

Another objection to the idea that I could be dreaming that I am writing this is that experience of dreams is very different from experience of waking life, and that we can in fact tell whether we are dreaming or not by examining the quality of our experience. Dreams involve many events that would be impossible in waking life; they are not usually so vivid as waking experience; they may be hazy, disjointed, impressionistic, bizarre, and so on. Besides, the whole sceptical argument relies on the ability to distinguish dreams from waking life: how else would I know that I have sometimes dreamt that I was awake when in fact I was asleep? This memory only makes sense if I had a way of telling that one experience was of being actually awake and another was of dreaming that I was awake.

The force of this reply depends very much on the individual's experience of dreams. Some people's dreams may be startlingly different from waking life. However, many people have at least some dreams which are indistinguishable from their everyday experience, and some people's experience of waking life, particularly when under the influence of alcohol or other drugs, may have a strong dream-like quality. Also the experience of false awakenings – when the dreamer dreams that he or she has woken up, got out of bed, dressed, had breakfast, and so on – is relatively common. However, in such cases the dreamer does not usually question whether this is waking life or not. It is usually not until he or she actually wakes up that the question 'Am I dreaming now?' becomes relevant.

At least one philosopher, Norman Malcolm (1911–90), has argued that the concept of dreaming makes it logically impossible to ask the question 'Am I dreaming?' whilst in a dream. To ask a question implies that the person asking it is conscious. But, Malcolm maintains, when dreaming I am by definition not conscious, since I am asleep. If I am not asleep, I cannot be dreaming. If I can ask the question, I cannot be asleep, and so I cannot be dreaming. I can only dream that I am asking the question, and that is not the same as genuinely asking it.

However, research into dreaming has shown that many people experience different levels of consciousness during sleep. Some have what are known as lucid dreams. A lucid dream is one in which the dreamer becomes aware that he or she is dreaming, and yet continues to dream. The existence of such dreams refutes the idea that it is impossible to be both dreaming and conscious at the same time. The mistake that Malcolm made was to redefine 'dreaming' in such a way that it no longer meant what is generally understood by the term. It is too simple a view of a dream to say that it is necessarily a non-conscious state.

HALLUCINATION

Even if I am not dreaming, I may be hallucinating. Someone might have slipped a mind-altering drug into my coffee so that I seem to see things which aren't really there at all. Perhaps I haven't really got a pen in my hand; perhaps I'm not really sitting in front of a window on a sunny day. If no one has slipped LSD into my coffee, perhaps it's just that I have reached such a severe state of alcoholism that I have started to hallucinate. However, although this is a possibility, it is highly unlikely that I would be able to carry on my life so easily. If the chair on which I am sitting is only imaginary, how does it support my weight? One answer to this is that I might be hallucinating sitting down in the first place: I might think that I am about to lower myself into a comfortable armchair when in fact I am lying on a stone floor having just taken a hallucinogenic drug or having just drunk a whole bottle of Pernod.

The most extreme version of such scepticism about the external world and my relation to it is to imagine that I don't have a body at all. All I am is a brain floating around in a jar of chemicals. An evil scientist has wired up my brain in such a way that I have the illusion of sensory experience. The scientist has created a kind of experience machine. I can, as far as I'm concerned, get up and walk to the shops to buy a newspaper. However, when I do this all that is really happening is that the scientist is stimulating certain of the nerves in my brain so that I have the illusion of doing this. All of the experience which I think is coming in through my five senses is in fact a result of this evil scientist stimulating my disembodied brain. With this experience machine the scientist can cause me to have any sensory experience that I could have in real life. Through a complex stimulation of the nerves in my brain the scientist can give me the illusion that I am watching television, running a marathon, writing a book, eating pasta, or anything else that I might do. This situation is not as far-fetched as it might sound: scientists are already experimenting with computer simulations of experience known as 'virtual reality' machines.

The story of the evil scientist is an example of what philosophers call a thought experiment. This is an imaginary situation which is described in order to make clear to us certain features of our concepts and everyday assumptions. In a thought experiment, as in a scientific experiment, by eliminating complicating details and by controlling what goes on, the philosopher can make discoveries about the concepts under investigation. In this case the thought experiment is designed to show some of the assumptions we typically make about the causes of our experience. Is there anything about my experience which could show that this thought experiment doesn't give a true picture of reality, that I am not simply a brain in a jar in a corner of an evil scientist's laboratory?

MEMORY AND LOGIC

Whilst the idea that I might be just a brain in a jar seems to be an extreme form of scepticism, there are in fact still further assumptions which can be called into doubt. All of the arguments we have discussed so far presuppose that memory is more or less reliable. When we say that we remember our senses being unreliable in the past, we assume that these memories really are memories, that they are not just the products of our imagination or wishful thinking. And every argument which uses words assumes that we have correctly remembered the meaning of the words used. Yet memory, just like the evidence of our senses, is notoriously unreliable. Just as all my experience is compatible with the view that I might be a brain in a jar being stimulated by an evil scientist, so, as Bertrand Russell (1872–1970) pointed out, it is compatible with the view that the world could have come into existence five minutes ago with everyone in it with 'memories' intact, all remembering an entirely unreal past.

However, if we start seriously to question the reliability of memory, then we make all communication impossible: if we can't assume that our memories of the meanings of words are generally reliable, then there is no way we can even discuss scepticism. Also, it could plausibly be argued that the thought experiment of the evil scientist manipulating the brain in a jar already introduces a scepticism about the reliability of memory, since presumably it is within the power of our tormentor to make us believe that words mean anything he or she chooses them to mean.

A second sort of assumption which sceptics rarely call into doubt is the reliability of logic. If sceptics were to call into question whether logic is really reliable, then this would undermine their position. Sceptics use arguments which rely on logic: their aim is not to contradict themselves. Yet, if they use logical arguments to prove that nothing is immune to doubt, then this means that their logical arguments themselves may not hold. So, by using arguments at all, sceptics seem to be relying heavily on something which, to be consistent, they would have to say is itself uncertain.

However, these objections do not answer the Illusion Argument, they only suggest that scepticism has limits; there are some assumptions which even an extreme sceptic has to make.

I THINK THEREFORE I AM

If this is so, is there nothing about which I can be certain? The most famous, and most important, answer to this sceptical question was given by Descartes. He argued that even if all my experience was the product of someone or something deliberately deceiving me – he used the idea of an evil demon rather than an evil scientist – the very fact that I was being deluded would show me something certain. It would show me that I exist, since if I did not exist there would be nothing for the deceiver to deceive. This argument is often known as the Cogito, from the Latin 'Cogito ergo sum', which means 'I think therefore I am'.

CRITICISM OF THE COGITO

Some people have found the Cogito argument convincing. Yet its conclusions are extremely limited. Even if we accept that the fact that I am thinking at all proves that I exist, it says nothing about what I am, apart from a thinking thing.

In fact some philosophers, including A. J. Ayer, have argued that even this goes too far. Descartes was wrong to have used the words 'I think': if he was to have been consistent with his general sceptical approach, he should have said 'there are thoughts'. He was making the assumption that if there are thoughts then there must be a thinker. But this is open to doubt. Perhaps thoughts could exist independently of thinkers. Perhaps it is just the way our language is structured which leads us to believe that every thought needs a thinker. The 'I' in 'I think' may be of the same kind as the 'It' in 'It is raining', which does not refer to anything.

REPRESENTATIVE REALISM

We have come a long way from considering the position of common-sense realism. In following through sceptical arguments about the senses, and about the question of whether we could be dreaming, we have seen the scope and limits of this type of philosophical doubt. In the process we have discovered some of the limitations of common-sense realism. In particular the Illusion Argument showed that the assumption that the senses almost always give us true information about the nature of the external world is implausible. The fact that our senses can so easily mislead us should be enough to reduce our confidence in the view that objects really are as they seem to us.

Representative realism is a modification of common-sense realism. It is called *representative* because it suggests that all perception is a result of awareness of inner representations of the external world. When I see a seagull I do not see it directly in the way that common-sense realism suggests. I have no direct sensory contact with the bird. Rather, what I am aware of is a mental representation, something like an inner picture, of the seagull. My visual experience is not directly of the seagull, though it is caused by it, but rather it is experience of the representation of the seagull my senses produce.

Representative realism provides a response to objections raised by the Illusion Argument. Take the example of colour. The same dress can look very different when viewed under different lights: it might look anything from scarlet to black. If we were to examine the fibres of the dress material more closely we would probably find them to be a mixture of colours. How it is perceived will also depend upon the viewer: someone who is colour-blind might well see it differently from the way that I would see it. In view of these observations, it doesn't seem to make sense to say the dress is really red: its redness is not independent of the perceiver. In order to explain this kind of phenomenon, representative realism introduces the notion of primary and secondary qualities.

PRIMARY AND SECONDARY QUALITIES

John Locke (1632–1704) used this notion of primary and secondary qualities. Primary qualities are qualities which an object actually has, regardless of the conditions under which it is being perceived, or of whether it is being perceived at all. Primary qualities include size, shape, and movement. All objects, no matter how small, have these qualities, and, according to Locke, our mental representations of these qualities closely resemble those in the objects. Science is particularly concerned with the primary qualities of physical objects. The texture of an object, which is determined by its primary qualities, gives rise to our experience of secondary qualities.

Secondary qualities include colour, smell, and taste. It may seem as if these are really in the objects we perceive, so that the redness is somehow part of a red dress. But, in fact, what redness is is a power to produce red images in a normal viewer under normal conditions. Redness isn't part of a red dress in the way that its shape is. Ideas of secondary qualities don't resemble the actual objects, but, rather, are in part a product of the kind of sensory system we happen to have. According to representative realists, when we see a red dress, we see a mental image which matches up in some ways with the real dress that gives rise to the image. The redness of the red dress (a secondary quality of the dress) in the image does not resemble actual qualities in the real dress; however, the shape of the dress (a primary quality of the dress) in the image does typically resemble that of the real dress.

CRITICISMS OF REPRESENTATIVE REALISM

PERCEIVER IN THE HEAD

One criticism of representative realism is that it seems just to push the problem of understanding perception back one stage. According to representative realism, when we perceive anything we do it via some kind of mental representation. So seeing someone coming towards me is like watching a film of this happening. But if this is so, then what is it that is interpreting the image on the screen? It is as if I have a little person sitting in my head interpreting what is going on. And presumably this little person would have to have a smaller one inside interpreting the interpretation: and so on to infinity. It seems unlikely that I have an infinite number of little interpreters (sometimes referred to as *homunculi*) in my head.

THE REAL WORLD IS UNKNOWABLE

A major objection to representative realism is that it makes the real world unknowable. Or rather it is only knowable indirectly. All we can ever experience are our mental representations of the world, and we have no way of comparing these with the actual world. It is as if each of us is trapped in a private cinema which we are never allowed to leave. On the screen we see various films, and we assume that they show the real world as it actually is – at least in terms of the primary qualities of objects we see represented. But, as we cannot go outside the cinema to check on our assumption, we can never be sure just how close the resemblance between the world shown in the films and the actual world is.

This is a particular problem for representative realism because this theory states that our mental representations of the primary qualities of objects resemble the actual qualities of objects in the external world. But, if we have no way of checking to see this is true, we have no reason to believe it. If my mental representation of a coin is circular, I have no way in which to check that this corresponds to the actual shape of the coin. I am limited to the evidence of my senses, and, since these work by means of mental representations, I can never have direct information about the coin's actual properties.

IDEALISM

Idealism is a theory which avoids some of the difficulties which arise for representative realism. Like the latter theory, idealism makes sensory input the basic ingredient in our experience of the world. So it too is based on the notion that all our experience is of mental representations rather than of the world. However, idealism goes one step further than representative realism. It argues that there is no justification for saying that the external world exists at all, since, as we have seen in our criticisms of representative realism, it is unknowable.

This sounds absurd. How could anyone seriously argue that we are mistaken to talk about an external world? Surely all the evidence points in the opposite direction. An idealist would answer that physical objects – St Paul's Cathedral, my desk, other people, and so on – only exist while they are being perceived. We don't need to introduce the idea that there is a real world beyond our experience: all we can ever know about is our experiences. It is more convenient to say 'I can see my guitar over there' rather than 'I am having a guitar-type visual experience', but an idealist would argue that the former is just a kind of shorthand for the latter. The words 'my guitar' are a convenient way of referring to a repeated pattern of sense experiences, not to any physical object which exists independently of my perceptions. We are all locked in individual cinemas watching films, but there is no real world outside the cinemas. We cannot leave because there is nothing outside. The films are our only reality. When no one is watching the screen, the projector light is switched off but the film keeps on running through the projector. Whenever I look at the screen, the light comes on again and the film is at precisely the place it would have been had it been projected all along.

A consequence of this is that, for the idealist, objects only exist as long as they are being perceived. When an object is not being projected on to my private cinema screen, it no longer exists. Bishop Berkeley (1685–1753), the most famous idealist, declared that 'esse est percipi': 'to exist is to be perceived'. So when I leave a room it ceases to exist, when I shut my eyes the world disappears, when I blink whatever is in front of me is no longer there – provided, of course, no one else is perceiving these things at the time.

CRITICISMS OF IDEALISM

HALLUCINATIONS AND DREAMS

At first glance this theory of perception might have difficulty dealing with hallucinations and dreams. If all we ever experience are our own ideas, how can we distinguish between reality and imagination?

However, the idealist can explain this. Actual physical objects are, according to the idealist, repeated patterns of sensory information. My guitar is a pattern of sensory information which recurs in pre-dictable ways. My visual guitar-experiences fit in with my tactile guitar-experiences: I can see my guitar leaning against the wall, and then go and touch it. My guitar-experiences relate to each other in a regular way. If I were having a hallucination of a guitar, then there would not be such an interrelation between my experiences: perhaps when I went to play it I would not have the expected tactile experiences. Perhaps my visual guitar-experiences would behave in completely unpredictable ways: my guitar would seem to materialize and dissolve in front of me.

Similarly, an idealist can explain how we can distinguish between dreams and waking life in terms of the different ways in which sense experiences connect up with each other. In other words, it is not just the nature of an immediate experience which identifies whether it is a hallucination, a dream, or a real-life experience, but also its relation to other experiences: the general context of the experience.

LEADS TO SOLIPSISM

A major criticism of the idealist's theory of perception is that it seems to lead to solipsism: the view that all that exists is my mind, and that everything else is a creation of my own invention. If the only things which I can experience are my own ideas, not only does this lead to the view that there are no physical objects, but also that there are no other people (see the section 'Other Minds' in Chapter 7, pp. 153–156). I have just as much evidence for the existence of other people as I have for the existence of other physical objects, namely repeated patterns of sensory information. But then, since we have ruled out the idea that there are actual physical objects causing my experience, perhaps nothing exists except as an idea in my mind. Perhaps the whole world and everything in it is a creation of my mind. Perhaps no one else exists. To put it in terms of my example of the cinema: perhaps my own private cinema with its particular repertoire of films is the only thing which exists. There are no other cinemas, and there is nothing outside my cinema.

Why should it be a criticism of a theory that it leads to solipsism? One answer to this is that solipsism is closer to a mental illness, a form of megalomania, than a tenable philosophical position. Perhaps a more persuasive answer, one used by Jean-Paul Sartre in his book *Being and Nothingness*, is that in almost every action we all of us suggest that we believe that there are minds other than our own. In other words, it is not the kind of position which any of us could easily adopt at will: we are so used to assuming that other people exist that to behave consistently as a solipsist would be scarcely conceivable. Take the example of such social emotions as shame and embarrassment. If I am caught doing something which I would rather not be seen to be doing, such as peeping through someone's keyhole, I will very probably feel shame. Yet, if I were a solipsist, this would be nonsensical. The concept of shame itself would be meaningless. As a solipsist I would believe that I was the only mind in existence: there would be no one else to judge me. Similarly, to feel embarrassment as a solipsist would be absurd. There would be no one to feel embarrassed in front of except myself. The degree to which we are all committed to a belief in the existence of a world beyond our own experiences is such that to show that a philosophical position leads to solipsism is enough to undermine its plausibility.

SIMPLEST EXPLANATION

Idealism can also be criticized on other grounds. Even if we agree with the idealist that all we ever have access to is our own sense experiences, we might still want to know what causes these experiences and why they follow such regular patterns. Why is it that sense experiences can be arranged so easily into what we in everyday language call 'physical objects'? Surely the most straightforward answer to this is that physical objects actually exist out there in the external world, and that they cause our sense experiences of them. This is what Samuel Johnson (1709–84) no doubt meant when in response to Bishop Berkeley's idealism he kicked a large stone very hard and declared 'I refute it thus'.

Berkeley suggested that it is God, not physical objects, who causes our sense experience. God has given us ordered sense experience. God perceives every object all the time, so the world continues to exist when it is unperceived by humans. However, as we have seen in Chapter 1, the existence of God cannot be taken for granted. For many people the existence of actual physical objects would be a far more acceptable hypothesis as an explanation of the causes of our experience.

The idealist believes that for something to exist it must be perceived. One reason for the belief is that it is logically impossible for anyone to check to see if the contrary is the case: no one could observe whether my guitar ceases to exist when no one is perceiving it since in order to make the observation someone would have to perceive it. Yet even if this is so, there is a large amount of evidence which points to the fact that my guitar does continue to exist unperceived. The simplest explanation of why my guitar is still leaning against the wall when I wake up in the morning is that no one has moved, borrowed, or stolen it, and it has continued to exist unperceived throughout the night. The theory of phenomenalism is a development of idealism which takes this highly plausible hypothesis into account.

PHENOMENALISM

Like idealism, phenomenalism is a theory of perception based upon the idea that we only ever have direct access to sense experience, never to the external world. Where it differs from idealism is in its account of physical objects. Whereas idealists argue that our notion of a physical object is a shorthand for a group of sense experiences, phenomenalists such as John Stuart Mill think that physical objects can be described purely in terms of patterns of actual and *possible* sense experiences. The possibility of sense experience of my guitar continues even when I am not actually looking at it or touching it. Phenomenalists believe that all descriptions of physical objects can be translated into descriptions of actual or hypothetical sense experiences.

The phenomenalist is like someone trapped in their own private cinema, watching films. But, unlike the idealist, who believes that the things represented on the screen cease to exist when they are no longer being shown, the phenomenalist thinks that these objects continue to exist as possible experiences even though they are not being projected on to the screen at that moment. What is more, the phenomenalist believes that everything that appears, or might appear, on the screen can be described in the language of sense experience without any reference to physical objects.

Phenomenalism can be criticized in the following ways.

CRITICISMS OF PHENOMENALISM

DIFFICULTY OF DESCRIBING OBJECTS

It is extremely complicated to express a physical object statement such as 'my guitar is leaning against the wall in my bedroom, unperceived' solely in terms of sense experiences. In fact, all attempts to describe physical objects in this way have failed.

SOLIPSISM AND THE PRIVATE LANGUAGE ARGUMENT

Phenomenalism, like idealism, seems to lead to solipsism: other people are just actual or possible perceptual experiences that I might have. We have already examined several objections to solipsism; the Private Language Argument, an argument originally used by Ludwig Wittgenstein (1889–1951) in his book *Philosophical Investigations*, provides a further objection to this aspect of phenomenalism.

Phenomenalism assumes that each person can identify and name particular sensations solely on the basis of his or her own direct experience. This identification and re-identification of sensation relies on private experience, not on the existence of public physical objects. The Private Language Argument shows that such a private naming and re-identification of sensations could not possibly occur, and so undermines phenomenalism.

All language depends on rules, and rules depend on there being ways of checking that they have been correctly applied. Now, suppose a phenomenalist has a red sensation: how can he or she check that this sensation is the same colour as the others he or she has labelled 'red'? There is no way of checking this since there is, for the phenomenalist, little between its being red and his or her thinking it is red. It is like someone trying to remember the time of a train and having to check this memory against itself rather than against the real timetable. It is a private check, not a public one, and cannot be used to make sure that our public use of the word 'red' is correct. So the assumption that a phenomenalist could describe his or her experience in this self-certifying language is a mistaken one.

CAUSAL REALISM

Causal realism assumes that the causes of our sense experience are physical objects in the external world. Causal realism takes as its starting point the observation that the main biological function of our senses is to help us find our way around our environment. It is through our senses that we acquire beliefs about our environment. According to causal realism, when I see my guitar what actually happens is that light rays reflected from the guitar cause certain effects on my retina and on other areas of my brain. This leads to me acquiring certain beliefs about what I am seeing. The experience of acquiring the beliefs is the experience of seeing my guitar.

The route by which we acquire perceptual beliefs is important: not just any route will do. For me actually to see my guitar it is essential that my guitar is the cause of the beliefs I acquire about it. The appropriate causal link for seeing is that brought about by an object reflecting light rays on to my retina and the subsequent processing of this information in my brain. If, for example, I was under the influence of drugs and was merely hallucinating, then this would not be a case of seeing my guitar. The drug rather than the guitar would have been the cause of my beliefs.

Seeing is a matter of acquiring information about my surroundings. Like representative realism, causal realism assumes that there really is an external world which continues to exist whether or not it is being experienced. It also assumes that the beliefs we acquire through our sense organs are generally true – that is why as a result of natural selection in the course of evolution our sense receptors are as they are: they tend to give us reliable information about our environment.

Another great advantage of causal realism over rival theories of perception is that it can easily explain the fact that our existing knowledge affects what we perceive. In acquiring information our system of classification, and our existing knowledge, directly affect how we treat incoming information and what we select and interpret as relevant. We will return to this in the section on 'Observation' in the next chapter (see pp. 123 125).

CRITICISMS OF CAUSAL REALISM

EXPERIENCE OF SEEING

The main criticism of causal realism is that it doesn't take adequate account of what it is actually like to see something, the qualitative aspect of sight. It reduces the experience of perceiving to a form of information gathering. However, causal realism is the most satisfactory theory of perception to date.

ASSUMES REAL WORLD

Causal realism makes the assumption that there is a real world out there that exists independently of people perceiving it. This is what is known as a metaphysical assumption – in other words it is an assumption about the nature of reality. Someone of idealist tendencies would find this metaphysical assumption unacceptable. However, since most of us are committed to a belief that there is a real world that exists independently of us, this assumption can be seen as a point in favour of causal realism, rather than as a criticism of it.

CONCLUSION

In this chapter we have explored some of the major philosophical theories about the external world and our relation to it. The next chapter concentrates on one particular way of finding out about the world, namely by scientific investigation.

FURTHER READING

René Descartes's sceptical arguments are presented in the first of his *Meditations* and his Cogito argument is at the beginning of the second. These are both in *Descartes: Meditations on First Philosophy* (revised edition, Cambridge: Cambridge University Press, 1996), an edition that includes introductions by John Cottingham and Bernard Williams. By far the best short introduction to Descartes's philosophy is Bernard Williams's interview in *The Great Philosophers*, edited by Bryan Magee (Oxford: Oxford University Press, 1987), a book I have already recommended.

Stephen Priest's *The British Empiricists* (Harmondsworth: Penguin, 1990) includes discussion of many of the topics in this chapter.

Adam Morton's *A Guide Through the Theory of Knowledge* (2nd edition, Oxford: Blackwell, 1997) is a clear introduction to epistemology. A. J. Ayer's *The Problem of Knowledge* (Harmondsworth: Penguin, 1956) is useful, if a little dated.

Bertrand Russell's *The Problems of Philosophy* (Oxford: Oxford University Press, 1912) is still well worth reading: it is a short introduction to philosophy, concentrating on epistemological questions, which was recommended reading for those thinking of studying philosophy at university for most of the twentieth century.

6

SCIENCE

Science has allowed us to send people to the moon, to cure tuberculosis, to invent the atom bomb, the motor car, the aeroplane, television, computers, and numerous other devices which have changed the nature of our everyday life. Scientific method is generally recognized as the most effective way we have of finding out about and predicting the behaviour of the natural world. Not all scientific inventions have been beneficial to human beings – obviously scientific developments have been used to destroy as well as improve human life. However, it would be difficult to deny the successful manipulations of the natural world which science has made possible. Science has produced results, whereas witchcraft, magic, superstition, and mere tradition have had little to show for themselves in comparison.

Scientific method is a great advance on previous ways of acquiring knowledge. Historically, science replaced 'truth by authority'. Truth by authority meant accepting as true the views of various important 'authorities' – notably the surviving works of the Ancient Greek philosopher Aristotle (384–322 BC), and the teachings of the Church – not because of what was claimed, but because of who claimed it. In contrast, scientific method emphasized the need to conduct tests, and to make detailed observations of the results before having confidence in any claim.

But what is this scientific method? Is it really as reliable as we are commonly led to believe? How does science progress? These are the sorts of questions which philosophers of science ask. Here we will consider some general questions about the nature of scientific method.

THE SIMPLE VIEW OF SCIENTIFIC METHOD

A simple, but widespread, view of scientific method is as follows. The scientist begins by making a large number of observations of some aspect of the world: for instance, the effect of heating water. These observations should be as objective as possible: the scientist aims to be unbiased and unprejudiced in recording data. Once the scientist has gathered a large amount of data based on observations, the next stage is to create a theory which explains the pattern of results. This theory, if it is a good one, will both explain what was happening, and predict what is likely to happen in the future. If future results do not quite fit with these predictions, then the scientist will usually modify the theory to cope with them. Because there is a great deal of regularity in the natural world, scientific predictions can be very accurate.

So, for instance, a scientist might begin by heating water to 100°C under normal conditions, and observe the water beginning to boil and evaporate. He or she may then make a number of further observations of the behaviour of water under different temperatures and pressures. On the basis of these observations the scientist will suggest a theory about the boiling point of water in relation to temperature and pressure. This theory will not only explain the particular observations that the scientist happened to make, but also, if it is a good theory, it will explain and predict all future observations of the behaviour of water under different temperatures and pressures. On this view scientific method begins with observation, moves to theory, and thus produces a generalization (or universal statement) with predictive ability. The generalization, if it is a good one, will be considered a law of nature. Science produces objective results which can be confirmed by anyone who wants to go out and repeat the original tests.

This view of scientific method is surprisingly widespread, even among practising scientists. Yet it is unsatisfactory in a number of ways. The most important of these are its assumptions about the nature of observation and about inductive argument.

CRITICISMS OF THE SIMPLE VIEW

OBSERVATION

As we have seen, the simple view of scientific method says that scientists begin by making unbiased observations before they formulate theories to explain those observations. This, however, is an inaccurate description of what observation is really like: the simple view assumes that our knowledge and expectations do not affect our observations, that it is possible to make observations in a completely unprejudiced way.

As I suggested when discussing perception in the previous chapter, seeing something isn't just having an image on your retina. Or, as the philosopher N. R. Hanson (1924–67) put it, 'There is more to seeing than meets the eyeball.' Our knowledge and our expectations of what we are likely to see affect what we actually do see. For instance, when I look at the wires of a telephone exchange, I see just a chaotic tangle of coloured wires; a telephone engineer looking at the same thing would see patterns of connections and so on. The telephone engineer's background of beliefs affects what he or she actually sees. It is not that the engineer and I have the same visual experience which we then go on to interpret differently: visual experience, as the causal realist theory of perception emphasizes, cannot be separated from our beliefs about what we are seeing.

As another example of this point, think of the difference between what a trained physicist sees when looking at an electron microscope, and what someone from a pre-scientific culture would see looking at the same equipment. The physicist would understand the interrelation between the different parts of the instrument, and would appreciate how to use it, and what could be done with it. To the person from the pre-scientific culture it would presumably be a meaningless jumble of odd bits of metal and wires, joined together in a mysterious way.

Of course, there is a great deal of overlap between what different viewers of the same scene will see, otherwise communication would be impossible. But the simple view of scientific method tends to neglect this important fact about observation: what we see cannot simply be reduced to the images on our retinas. What we see usually depends on what is called our 'mental set': our knowledge and expectations, and, for that matter, our cultural upbringing.

However, it is worth noting that there are some observations which obstinately refuse to be affected by our beliefs. Even though I know that the moon is no larger when it is lower on the horizon than it is when it is at its zenith, I can't help seeing it as larger. My perceptual experience of the moon, in this case, is unaffected by my conscious background beliefs. Obviously I would describe it as 'looking larger' rather than as 'being larger', and this involves theory, but this appears to be an instance where my perceptual experience remains immune to influence from my beliefs. What this shows is that the relation between what we know and what we see is not as straightforward as is sometimes supposed: background knowledge does not always cause us to see differently. This does not undermine the argument against the simple view of science, since in most cases what we see is significantly affected by our mental set.

OBSERVATION STATEMENTS

A second important feature of observation in a scientific context which the simple view neglects is the nature of observation statements. The scientist must express particular observations in language. Yet the language the scientist uses to make these observation statements always has theoretical assumptions built into it. There is no such thing as a completely neutral observation statement: observation statements are 'theory laden'. For example, even such an everyday statement as 'He touched the bare wire and gave himself an electric shock' assumes that there is such a thing as electricity and that it can be harmful. By using the word 'electric', the speaker presupposes a whole theory about the causes of the harm experienced by the person touching the wire. To understand the statement fully would involve understanding theories about both electricity and physiology. Theoretical assumptions are built into the way the event is described. In other words, observation statements classify our experience in a particular way, but this is not the only way we could classify our experience.

The sorts of observation statement actually made in science, such as 'the molecular structure of the material was affected by heating', presuppose quite elaborate theories. Theory always comes first: the simple view of scientific method is completely wrong to suppose that unbiased observation always precedes theory. What you see usually depends on what you know, and the words you choose to describe what you see always presuppose a theory of the nature of the thing you see. These are two inescapable facts about the nature of observation which undermine the notion of objective, unprejudiced, neutral observation.

SELECTION

A third point about observation is that scientists don't just 'observe', recording each and every measure of each and every phenomenon. That would be physically impossible. Scientists choose which aspects of any situation they concentrate on. This choice too involves decisions which are theory-related.

THE PROBLEM OF INDUCTION

A different sort of objection to the simple view of scientific method arises because it relies on induction rather than deduction. Induction and deduction are two different types of argument. An inductive argument typically involves a generalization based on a certain number of specific observations. If I were to make a large number of observations of animals with fur, and from these conclude that all animals with fur are viviparous (that is, they give birth to live young rather than laying eggs), I would be using an inductive argument. A deductive argument, on the other hand, begins with particular premises, and then moves logically to a conclusion which follows from those premises. For instance, I might conclude from the premises 'All birds are animals' and 'Swans are birds' that therefore all swans are animals: this is a deductive argument.

Deductive arguments are truth-preserving. This means that if their premises are true, then their conclusions *must* be true. You would contradict yourself if you asserted the premises but denied the conclusion. So if 'All birds are animals' and 'Swans are birds' are both true, then it must be true that all swans are animals. In contrast, the conclusions of inductive arguments with true premises may or may not be true. Even though every observation of animals with fur that I made was accurate, and the animals were all viviparous, and even though I made many thousands of observations, my inductive conclusion that all animals with fur are viviparous could still turn out to be false. In fact the existence of the duck-billed platypus, a peculiar fur-covered animal which lays eggs, means that it is a false generalization.

We use this sort of inductive argument all the time. I have drunk coffee many times, but it has never poisoned me, so I assume on the basis of the inductive argument that coffee will not poison me in the future. Day has always followed night in my experience, so I assume that it will continue to do so. I have observed many times that if I stand in the rain I get wet, so I assume the future will be like the past, and avoid standing out in the rain whenever possible. These are all examples of induction. Our whole lives are based on the fact that induction provides us with fairly reliable predictions about our environment and the probable results of our actions. Without the principle of induction, our interaction with our environment would be completely chaotic: we would have no basis for assuming that the future would be like the past. We would not know if the food we were about to eat would nourish or poison us; we would not know at each step whether the ground would support us or open up into a chasm, and so on. All predicted regularity in our environment would be open to doubt.

Despite this central part played by induction in all our lives, there is the undeniable fact that the principle of induction is not entirely reliable. As we have already seen, it could give us a false answer to the question of whether or not all fur-covered animals are viviparous. Its conclusions are not as reliable as those arising from deductive arguments with true premises. To illustrate this point, Bertrand Russell used the example of a chicken that wakes up every morning thinking that as it was fed the previous day, so it would be again that day. It wakes up one morning only to have its neck wrung by the farmer. The chicken was using an inductive argument based on a large number of observations. In relying so heavily on induction are we being as foolish as this chicken? How can we be justified in putting our faith in induction? This is the so-called Problem of Induction, a problem identified by David Hume in his *Treatise*

Concerning Human Nature. How can we ever justify relying on such an unreliable method of argument? This is of particular relevance to the philosophy of science, because, at least on the simple theory outlined above, induction has a crucial role to play in scientific method.

INFERENCE TO THE BEST EXPLANATION

Not all inductive arguments are of the form outlined above. Another important non-deductive style of arguing is known as Inference to the Best Explanation or, less commonly, abduction. With this sort of argument we don't simply move from past observation to general predictions for the future. Instead we judge the plausibility of a hypothesis in terms of the sort of explanation if offers. The best hypothesis is the one that explains more. So, for example, if I get home to find mouse entrails in the kitchen and my cat fast asleep looking very contented at the very time he usually demands to be fed, the best explanation of what happened in my absence is that my cat caught and ate a mouse and then took a nap. I see the evidence, but I don't *deduce* the conclusion: there are other possible explanations of what happened.

For instance, another cat might have come in through the cat door and left a mouse's entrails on the kitchen floor. Or perhaps my wife, trying to confuse me, has killed and dismembered a mouse and left it there to frame the cat. My conclusion that it was my cat that killed and ate the mouse is, however, the more plausible one in the circumstances. This is because, while the competing hypotheses can explain the entrails, they don't explain why the cat looks so contented. This style of reasoning is very important in science and in everyday life. But, as the above example shows, it is not completely reliable. There is always some other possible explanation of the same evidence. My wife might have framed the cat, and might just have picked a day on which the cat was particularly inactive and so slept through his usual dinnertime. The conclusion, then, with an Inference to the Best Explanation does not follow inevitably from the premises as it does with a valid deductive argument. This also raises all sorts of questions about what is to count as the best explanation in any circumstances and why.

Philosophers disagree as to whether or not Inference to the Best Explanation is best described as a form of induction. They do, however, all acknowledge that the truth of the premises of such an argument does not guarantee the truth of the conclusion. In this respect Inferences to the Best Explanation have none of the reliability of deductive arguments. This is not intended as a criticism of Inference to the Best Explanation. We use this style of reasoning in precisely the circumstances when deduction is impossible: when, for example, we are trying to understand the cause or explanation of something and there is more than one possible account of how things came to be as they are.

ANOTHER ASPECT OF THE PROBLEM OF INDUCTION

So far we have treated the Problem of Induction as just a question about the justification of generalizing about the future on the basis of the past. There is another aspect of the Problem of Induction which we have not yet touched upon. This is the fact that there are numerous very different generalizations we could make on the basis of the past, all of which are consistent with the available data. However, these different generalizations can give completely different predictions about the future. This is shown well in the philosopher Nelson Goodman's (1906–98) example of 'grue'. This example may seem somewhat contrived, but it illustrates an important point.

Goodman coined the term 'grue' to reveal this second aspect of the Problem of Induction. 'Grue' is an invented colour-word. Something is grue either if it is examined before the year 2000 and found to be green, or if it is not examined and is blue. Goodman was writing before 2000: in the discussion that follows, I have changed '2000' to '2100' to make his example work today. We have plenty of experience to suggest that the generalization 'All emeralds are green' is true. But our evidence is equally consistent with the view that 'All emeralds are grue' (assuming the observations are all made before the year 2100). Yet whether we say all emeralds are green or that they are all grue affects the predictions we will make about observations of emeralds after the year 2100. If we say that all emeralds are grue, then we will predict that some emeralds examined after the year 2100 will look blue. Those which have been examined before the year 2100 will be green in colour, and those which haven't been examined before the year 2100 will appear blue. If, however, as we are more likely to do, we say that all emeralds are green, then we will predict that they will all look green whenever they are examined.

What this example shows is that the predictions we make on the basis of induction are not the only ones we could make using the available evidence. So we are left with the conclusion not only that the predictions we make on the basis of induction are not 100 per cent reliable, but also that they are not even the only predictions consistent with the evidence we have accumulated.

ATTEMPTED SOLUTIONS TO THE PROBLEM OF INDUCTION

IT SEEMS TO WORK

One response to the Problem of Induction is to point out that reliance on induction is not only widespread, but reasonably fruitful: most of the time it is an extremely useful way of discovering regularities in, and predicting the future behaviour of, the natural world. As we have already noted, science has allowed us to send people to the moon; if science is based on the principle of induction, we have plenty of evidence that our faith in induction is justified. Of course there is always the possibility that the sun will not rise tomorrow, or that, like the chicken, we will wake up tomorrow to have our necks wrung, but induction is the best method we have. No other form of argument will help us predict the future better than the principle of induction.

An objection to this defence of the principle of induction is that the defence itself relies on induction. In other words, it is a viciously circular argument. What the argument amounts to is a claim that, because induction has proved successful in various ways in the past, it will continue to do so in the future. But this is itself a generalization based on a number of specific instances of induction working, and so it is itself an inductive argument. An inductive argument cannot provide a satisfactory justification of induction: that would be begging the question, presupposing what you are setting out to prove, namely that induction is justified.

EVOLUTION

Universal statements, that is statements which begin 'All …', such as 'All swans are white', presuppose similarity between the individual things which are being grouped together. In this case, there must be a similarity which all individual swans have for it to make sense to group them together. As we have seen in the case of 'grue', however, there is no one way in which we have to classify the things we find in the world or the properties we ascribe to them. It is possible that extraterrestrials landing on Earth would use very different categories from the ones we use, and on the basis of these make very different inductive predictions from those that we make.

Nevertheless, as the 'grue' example indicates, some generalizations seem more natural for us to make than others. The most plausible explanation for this is an evolutionary one: human beings are born with a genetically programmed group of categories into which we slot our experience. We have, as a species, by a process of natural selection, arrived at tendencies to make inductive generalizations which predict fairly accurately the behaviour of the world around us. It is these tendencies which come into play when we reason inductively: we have a natural tendency to group our experience of the world in ways which lead to reliable predictions. Whether or not this account of induction justifies our reliance on it, it does provide an explanation of why we generally trust inductive arguments, and why we are usually correct to do so.

PROBABILITY

Another response to the Problem of Induction is to admit that although we can never show the conclusion of an inductive argument to be 100 per cent certain, nevertheless we can show it to be very probably true. The so-called laws of nature which science discovers are not absolutely proven to hold: they are generalizations which have a high probability of being true. The more observations that we make confirming these laws, the more likely that they are true. This response is sometimes known as probabilism. We cannot say for certain that the sun will rise tomorrow, but we can, on the basis of induction, judge this to be highly likely.

However, an objection to this is that probability itself is something that can change. The assessment of the probability of an event occurring in the future is based on how frequently it has happened in the past. But the only justification for supposing that probability will hold in the future is itself inductive. So this is a circular argument since it relies on induction in order to justify our reliance on induction.

FALSIFICATIONISM: CONJECTURE AND REFUTATION

Another way out of the Problem of Induction, at least as it affects the issue of scientific method, is to deny that induction is the basis of scientific method. Falsificationism, the philosophy of science developed by Karl Popper (1902–94) amongst others, does just this. Falsificationists argue that the simple view of science is misguided. Scientists do not begin by making observations, they begin with a theory. Scientific theories, and so-called laws of nature, are not claims to truth: rather they are speculative attempts to give an analysis of various aspects of the natural world. They are conjectures: well-informed guesses, designed to improve upon previous theories.

These conjectures are then subjected to experimental testing. But this testing has a very specific aim. It is intended not so much to prove the conjecture true, but rather to prove that it is false. Science works by attempting to falsify theories rather than by proving them to be true. Any theory which is shown to be false is discarded or, at the very least, modified. Science thus progresses by means of conjecture and refutation. We cannot know for certain that any theory is absolutely true: any theory could in principle be falsified. This view seems to fit well with the progress witnessed in the history of science: the Ptolemaic view of the universe, which put the Earth at its centre, being superseded by the Copernican one; Newton's physics being superseded by Einstein's.

Falsification has at least one great advantage over the simple view of science. This is the fact that a single falsifying instance is enough to show that a theory is unsatisfactory, whereas no matter how many observations we make which confirm a theory, they can never be enough to give us 100 per cent certainty that the theory will hold for all future observations. This is a feature of universal statements. If I say, 'All swans are white' it only takes an observation of a single black swan to disprove my theory. Even if I observe two million white swans, the next swan I see could still be black: in other words, the generalization is far easier to disprove than to prove.

FALSIFIABILITY

Falsificationism also provides a way of discriminating between useful scientific hypotheses and hypotheses which are irrelevant to science. The test of the usefulness of a theory is the degree to which it is falsifiable. A theory is useless to science, indeed not really a scientific hypothesis at all, if no possible observation could falsify it. For instance, it is relatively straightforward to devise tests which could falsify the hypothesis 'The rain in Spain falls mainly on the plain', whereas there is no possible test to show that 'either it will rain today or it won't' is false. The latter statement is true by definition, and therefore nothing to do with empirical observation: it is not a scientific hypothesis.

The more falsifiable a statement is, the more useful it is to science. Many statements are expressed in vague ways, making it quite difficult to see how they could be tested, and how to interpret the results. A bold, falsifiable statement, however, will very quickly either be shown to be false, or else resist attempts at falsification. Either way it will help science to progress: if it is falsified, it will contribute by encouraging the development of a hypothesis which cannot so easily be refuted; if it proves difficult to falsify, it will provide a convincing theory, which any new theories will have to improve upon.

On close examination, some hypotheses which are widely thought to be scientific turn out to be untestable: there is no possible observation which would falsify them. One controversial example of this occurs in the case of psychoanalysis. Some falsificationists have argued that many of the claims of psychoanalysis are logically unfalsifiable, and therefore unscientific. If a psychoanalyst claims that a certain patient's dream is really about an unresolved sexual conflict from the patient's childhood, there is no observation which could possibly falsify this claim. If the patient denies that there was any conflict, the analyst will take this as further confirmation that the patient is repressing something. If the patient admits that the analyst's interpretation is correct, then this too will provide confirmation of the hypothesis. So there is no way in which to falsify the claim, and so it cannot increase our knowledge of the world. Therefore, according to the falsificationists, it is a pseudo-scientific hypothesis: not a real scientific hypothesis at all. However, just because a theory is not scientific in this sense, it does not follow that it is without value. Popper thought that many of the claims of psychoanalysis might eventually become testable, but in their pre-scientific form they should not be taken for scientific hypotheses.

The reason for avoiding untestable hypotheses in science is that they prevent science progressing: if there is no possibility of refuting them, then there is no way of replacing them with a better theory. The process of conjecture and refutation which is characteristic of the progress of science is thwarted. Science progresses through mistakes: through theories which are falsified and replaced by better ones. In this sense there is a certain amount of trial and error in science. Scientists try out a hypothesis, see whether they can falsify it, and if so replace it with a better one, which is then subjected to the same treatment. The hypotheses which are replaced – the mistakes – all contribute to the general increase in our knowledge about the world. In contrast, theories which are logically unfalsifiable are, in that form, of little use to the scientist.

Many of the most revolutionary scientific theories have originated from bold imaginative conjectures. Popper's theory emphasizes the creative imagination involved in thinking up new theories. In this it gives a more plausible explanation of creativity in science than does the simple view which makes scientific theories logical deductions from observations.

CRITICISMS OF FALSIFICATIONISM

ROLE OF CONFIRMATION

One criticism of falsificationism is that it fails to take into account the role of confirmation of hypotheses in science. By concentrating on attempts to falsify hypotheses, it plays down the effects of successful predictions on whether or not a scientific theory is accepted. For instance, if my hypothesis is that the temperature at which water boils varies in a constant way in relation to the atmospheric pressure at which the experiment is carried out, then this will allow me to make a number of predictions about the temperature at which water will boil at various pressures. It might lead me to predict – accurately – that mountaineers would not be able to make a good cup of tea at high altitudes because the water would boil at a temperature of less than 100°C and so the tea leaves would not infuse properly. If my predictions are shown to be accurate, this lends positive support to my theory. The sort of falsificationism described above ignores this aspect of science. Successful predictions on the basis of hypotheses, particularly if they are unusual and original hypotheses, play a significant role in scientific development.

This does not undermine falsificationism: the logical power of a single falsifying observation is still always greater than any number of confirming observations. Nevertheless, falsificationism needs to be adapted slightly to acknowledge the part played by the confirmation of hypotheses.

HUMAN ERROR

Falsificationism seems to advocate the overthrow of a theory on the basis of a single falsifying case. In practice, however, there are many components to any scientific experiment or study, and there is usually considerable scope for error and misinterpretation of results. Measuring devices may malfunction, or data collection methods may be unreliable. Surely, then, scientists should not be so easily swayed by one observation which appears to undermine a theory.

Popper would agree with this. It is not a serious problem for falsificationism. From a logical point of view it is clear that in principle a single falsifying instance could undermine a theory. However, Popper is not suggesting that practising scientists should simply abandon a theory as soon as they have an apparently falsifying case: they should be sceptical and investigate every possible source of error.

HISTORICALLY INACCURATE

Falsificationism does not adequately account for many of the most significant developments in the history of science. The Copernican Revolution, the recognition that the sun was at the centre of the universe and that the Earth and other planets orbited round it, illustrates the fact that the presence of apparently falsifying instances did not lead to major figures rejecting their hypotheses. Change in the scientific model of the nature of the universe did not occur through a process of conjecture followed by refutation. It was only after several centuries of development of physics that the theory could be adequately tested against observations.

Similarly, Isaac Newton's (1642–1727) theory of gravity was apparently falsified by observations of the moon's orbit, made soon after he had made his theory public. Only at a much later date were these observations shown to have been misleading. Despite this apparent refutation, Newton and others clung to the theory of gravity, and this had beneficial effects on the development of science. Yet, on Popper's falsificationist account, Newton's theory should have been discarded on the grounds that it had been falsified.

What these two examples suggest is that the falsificationist theory of science does not always fit well with the actual history of science. The theory at least needs modification to be able to explain accurately how scientific theories are superseded. The work of Thomas Kuhn (1922–95) suggests that what actually happens at key moments in the history of science is that a new paradigm is developed, a whole new framework within which science is conducted. At such a moment there is not a rational decision to jettison a refuted paradigm due to the weight of evidence against it. Radically new paradigms undermine the assumptions of the way science has been conducted up to that point: they involve new assumptions, new interpretations of evidence, and a new range of problems to be solved. Justification for the new paradigm doesn't emerge from within the framework of the old paradigm. Science does not progress by conjecture and refutation, but by a series of paradigm shifts.

SCIENTISM

Bold claims are often made for the scope of science. Some people have even argued that science can explain everything that is important about the human condition. If something can't be explained scientifically, they argue, it can't be explained at all. Some philosophers have even declared that philosophy itself is part of science. Similar ideas have taken root in other academic areas too, including the study of literature and music. The term 'scientism' is often used in a dismissive way to refer to a range of such views.

CRITICISM OF SCIENTISM

IMPOVERISHED ACCOUNT OF EXPLANATION

The sort of explanation that scientists aim at is general. Scientists seek law-like generalizations that apply in a wide range of situations. But to understand, for example, a particular relationship between two human beings in terms of physiological responses, genetic inheritance, childhood conditioning, and so on, though it might give an accurate picture, omits the lived experience of falling in (or out of) love – a topic which can be more readily addressed by a novelist or poet than an experimental psychologist. Similarly, those trying to understand a piece of music as listeners do not typically need the musicologist's complex analyses of harmony or the physiologist's account of hearing to appreciate the music. Scientific explanations have their place, but they are not everything. The main objection to scientism is that it overvalues scientific explanation.

CONCLUSION

In this chapter I have concentrated on the Problem of Induction and on the falsificationist account of scientific method. Although practising scientists need not be aware of the philosophical implications of what they are doing, many have been influenced by the falsificationist account of scientific progress. Even though philosophy does not necessarily affect the way scientists work, it can certainly change the way they understand their work.

FURTHER READING

A. F. Chalmers's *What Is This Thing Called Science?* (3rd edition, Milton Keynes: Open University Press, 1999) is an excellent introduction to this area: it is well written and stimulating. It covers most of the important issues in contemporary philosophy of science in an accessible way. C. G. Hempel's *Philosophy of Natural Science* (Englewood Cliffs, NJ: Prentice-Hall, 1966) and Samir Okasha's *Philosophy of Science: A Very Short Introduction* (Oxford: Oxford University Press, 2002) may also be found useful.

Bryan Magee's *Popper* (London: Fontana, 1973) is a good introduction to the work of Karl Popper. Thomas S. Kuhn's *The Structure of Scientific Revolutions* (3rd revised edition, Chicago: University of Chicago Press, 1996) is an important, influential, and readable contribution to the philosophy of science.

John Losee's *A Historical Introduction to the Philosophy of Science* (3rd edition, Oxford: Oxford University Press, 1993) provides a clear and interesting survey of the history of the philosophy of science.

MIND

7

What is the mind? Do we have non-physical souls? Is thought simply an aspect of physical matter, just a by-product of nerves being stimulated in the brain? How can we be sure that other people aren't just sophisticated robots? How can we tell that they are actually conscious? All these questions fall into the category of philosophy of mind.

PHILOSOPHY OF MIND AND PSYCHOLOGY

Philosophy of mind should be distinguished from psychology, although they are quite closely related. Psychology is the scientific study of human behaviour and thought: it is based on observation of people, often under experimental conditions. In contrast, philosophy of mind is not an experimental subject: it does not involve making actual scientific observations. Philosophy concentrates on the analysis of our concepts.

Philosophers of mind are concerned with conceptual issues which arise when we think about the mind. A psychologist might investigate schizophrenia by examining patients, running tests on them, and so on. A philosopher on the other hand would ask conceptual questions like 'What is the mind?' or 'What do we mean by "mental illness"?' Such questions cannot be answered by examination of actual cases alone: they require us to analyse the meaning of the terms in which they are expressed.

To illustrate this point, consider another example. A neuropsychologist investigating human thought might make observations of the patterns of nerve stimulation in the brain. A philosopher of mind would ask the more basic conceptual question of whether the activity of these nerves amounts to thinking, or whether there is some feature of our concept of thought which means that it cannot be reduced to a physical occurrence. Or, to put it in a more traditional way, do we have minds distinct from our bodies?

In this chapter we will examine some of the central debates in the philosophy of mind, concentrating on the question of whether a physical explanation of the mind is adequate, and on whether we can have knowledge of other people's minds.

THE MIND/BODY PROBLEM

In the way we describe ourselves and the world we usually make a distinction between the mental and physical aspects. Mental aspects are such things as thinking, feeling, deciding, dreaming, imagining, wishing, and so on. Physical ones include feet, limbs, our brains, cups of tea, the Empire State Building, and so on.

When we do something, such as play tennis, we use both our mental and our physical aspects: we think about the rules of the game, where our opponent is likely to play the next shot, and so on, and we move our bodies. But is there a real division between mind and body, or is this just a convenient way of talking about ourselves? The problem of explaining the true relationship between mind and body is known as the Mind/Body Problem.

Those who believe that mind and body are separate things, that each of us has both a mind and a body, are called mind/body dualists. Those who believe that the mental is in some sense the same thing as the physical, that we are nothing more than flesh and blood and have no separate mind substance, are known as physicalists.

ZOMBIES

There is a lot at stake here. Imagine that it is possible to make a perfect copy of your body that matches every molecule. A physicalist would have to say that your artificial twin would experience consciousness just as you do. A dualist, in contrast, could allow that even though there are no physical differences between you there may be mental ones. In an extreme case your artificial twin might act in just the same sorts of ways as you, come out with the same sorts of comment in the same accent, but actually have no inner life. Your twin might be a kind of zombie. This zombie does all the sorts of things you do, says 'ouch!' when it burns itself, for instance, but doesn't actually feel pain.

This is obviously a far-fetched example, and no one is suggesting that some people are zombies of this kind. The point of it is to bring out the very different assumptions of physicalists and dualists. In principle, for dualists mind and body can separate. Dualists can make sense of the thought experiment. For physicalists there can be no zombies of this kind: they believe that anyone who shares your structure molecule for molecule will have the same sort of inner life as you, will experience consciousness as you do.

DUALISM

Dualism, as we have seen, involves a belief in the existence of a non-physical substance: the mental. A dualist typically believes that body and mind are distinct substances which interact with each other but remain separate. Mental processes, such as thinking, are not the same as physical ones, such as brain cells firing; mental processes occur in the mind, not in the body. The mind is not the living brain.

Mind/body dualism is a view held by many people, particularly by those who believe that it is possible to survive our bodily death, either by living in some kind of spirit world or by being reincarnated in a new body. Both these views presuppose that human beings are not just physical beings, but rather that our most important part is the non-physical mind or, as it is more often called in religious contexts, the soul. René Descartes is probably the most famous mind/body dualist: such dualism is often called Cartesian dualism ('Cartesian' being the adjective formed from Descartes's name).

A strong motive for believing dualism to be true is the difficulty most of us have in seeing how a purely physical thing, such as the brain, could give rise to the complex patterns of feeling and thought which we call consciousness. How could something purely physical feel melancholy, or appreciate a painting? Such questions give dualism an initial plausibility as a solution to the Mind/Body Problem. However, there are a number of powerful criticisms of it as a theory.

CRITICISMS OF DUALISM

CANNOT BE SCIENTIFICALLY INVESTIGATED

One criticism sometimes levelled at mind/body dualism is that it does not really help us to understand the nature of the mind. All it tells us is that there is a non-physical substance in each of us which thinks, dreams, experiences, and so on. But, it is alleged by physicalists, a non-physical mind couldn't be investigated directly: in particular, it couldn't be investigated scientifically because science only deals with the physical world. All we could examine would be its effects on the world.

Against this the dualist might reply that we can observe the mind through introspection, that is, through considering our own thought. And we can and do investigate the mind indirectly through its effects on the physical world. Most science works by inferring the causes of observed effects; scientific investigation of a non-physical mind would be an instance of this same type of approach. Besides which, mind/body dualism at least has the benefit of explaining how it might be possible to survive bodily death, something which physicalism cannot do without introducing the idea of the resurrection of the body after death.

EVOLUTION

It is generally accepted that human beings evolved from simpler life forms. However, a dualist will find it difficult to explain how this could have been so. Presumably very simple life forms such as amoebae do not have minds, whereas human beings, and probably some of the higher animals, do have them. How then could amoebae give rise to creatures which have minds? Where could this mind substance have suddenly come from? And why does the evolution of mind so closely parallel the evolution of the brain?

One way in which a dualist could answer this criticism is to say that even amoebae have minds of a very limited sort, and that the mind evolved in parallel with the evolution of animal bodies. Or the dualist could go a step further and say that every physical thing also has a mind of some sort: this last view is known as pan-psychism. According to panpsychists even stones have very primitive minds. The development of human mental ability can then be explained in terms of its being a combination of physical substances and thus a merging of simple minds to create a more complex one. However, few dualists are sympathetic to such an approach, partly because it blurs the distinction between human beings and what we consider to be the inanimate world.

INTERACTION

The most serious difficulty the dualist faces is that of explaining how two such different substances as mind and body could possibly interact. It is clear, in the dualist view, that, for example, I can have a thought and then this thought can give rise to a bodily move-ment. For instance, I can think that I will scratch my nose, and then my finger moves up to my nose and scratches it. The difficulty for the dualist is to show precisely how the purely mental thought can lead to the physical scratch.

This difficulty is made more pronounced by the fact that events in the brain are very closely linked with mental events. Why do we need to introduce the idea of the mind as distinct from the body when it is obvious that, for example, severe damage to the brain leads to mental deficiency? If mind and body are really distinct, why is this so?

CONTRADICTS A BASIC SCIENTIFIC PRINCIPLE

Another aspect of the difficulty of explaining interaction is that it seems to contradict a very basic principle of science. Most scientists, particularly those who are physicalists, assume that every change in an object can be explained by a prior physical event: the causes of all physical events are themselves physical. So, for instance, if a nerve cell in someone's brain fires, a neuropsychologist will look for a physical cause of this. But if pure thought, which is an activity of the mind, can lead to action, then some merely mental events must directly lead to physical ones. Dualists are left having to justify revising quite a basic assumption of science. Of course, they may feel that they can justify this revision on the grounds that dualism is self-evidently true; but, if there is any doubt about this, it seems more sensible to assume that it is the theory of dualism that is at fault, and not the scientific assumption which has produced such fruitful results in scientific research to date.

DUALISM WITHOUT INTERACTION

MIND/BODY PARALLELISM

One way in which the dualist can get round the problems associated with explaining how mind/body interaction is possible is to deny that it occurs at all. Some dualists have argued that although both mind and body exist, and we all have one of each, there is no actual interaction between them. This slightly strange idea is known as psychophysical parallelism. Mind and body run in parallel like two clocks which have been set to the same time. When someone stands on my toe I feel a pain, but not because I get any message from my body to my mind. It is simply that God (or else a quite staggering cosmological coincidence) has set the two independent aspects of me running in parallel. At the time someone treads on my toe it has been so arranged that I feel pain in my mind, but the one event does not cause the other: it's just that they occur one immediately after the other.

OCCASIONALISM

Another equally strange attempt to explain how mind and body can interact is known as occasionalism. Whilst parallelism declares the apparent link between mind and body to be an illusion, occasionalism allows that there really is a link, but argues that this is provided by the intervention of God. God supplies the connection between mind and body, between my toe being injured and my feeling pain, or between my deciding to scratch my nose and my hand moving.

A major problem with mind/body parallelism, at least in its most plausible form, and with occasionalism, is that they both assume that God exists, something which, as we have seen in Chapter 1, is by no means self-evident. Moreover, even Theists are likely to find these theories a little far-fetched.

EPIPHENOMENALISM

A third approach to the problem of interaction is known as epiphenomenalism. This is the view that, although events in the body cause mental events, mental events never cause physical ones, nor do they give rise to other mental ones. The mind is, then, an epiphenomenon: in other words it is something which does not directly affect the body in any way. The epiphenomenalist explains my apparent ability to raise my hand by thinking about it as an illusion. Raising my hand is a purely physical action which only seems to be caused by my thought. All mental events are directly caused by physical ones, but no mental events give rise to physical ones.

Like parallelism and occasionalism, epiphenomenalism has little plausibility as a theory of mind. It raises as many difficult questions as it answers. Not least of the problems associated with it is that it makes free will an impossibility: we can never really choose to act, all we can have is an illusion of acting from choice. And why does causation take place only in one direction, physical causes having mental effects, but never vice versa?

PHYSICALISM

Having examined mind/body dualism and a number of criticisms and variants of it, let's now take a look at physicalism. Physicalism is the view that mental events can be completely explained in terms of physical ones, usually events in the brain. In contrast to mind/body dualism, which states that there are two basic sorts of substance, physicalism is a form of monism: it is the view that there is just one sort of substance, the physical. An immediate advantage of physicalism over dualism is that it suggests a programme for the scientific study of the mind. In theory at least it should be possible to give an entirely physical description of any mental event.

Physicalist philosophers do not try to discover precisely how particular brain states match up with thoughts: that is a task for neuropsychologists and other scientists. Such philosophers are mainly concerned to prove that all mental events are physical, and that dualism is therefore false.

There are several varieties of physicalism, some more open to criticism than others.

TYPE-IDENTITY THEORY

This variety of physicalism states that mental events are identical with physical ones. A thought about the weather, for example, is simply a particular state of the brain. Whenever this particular state of the brain occurs, then we can describe this as having a thought about the weather. This is known as type-identity theory. All physical states of a particular type are also mental ones of a particular type.

To make this view clearer, consider how the terms 'water' and 'H_2O' both refer to the same substance. We use the term 'water' in everyday contexts, and 'H_2O' in scientific ones. Now, whilst both terms refer to the same thing, they have slightly different meanings: 'water' is used to draw attention to the substance's basic properties of wetness and so on; 'H_2O' is used to reveal its chemical composition. Few people ask for a jug of H_2O to add to their whisky, yet water is H_2O: they are one and the same thing.

Similarly a flash of lightning is also an electrical discharge of a certain kind. Whether we use 'flash of lightning' or 'electrical discharge' to describe this event depends on whether we are caught in a thunderstorm or giving a more scientific analysis of what is going on. We can use the everyday term 'lightning' without having any awareness of the scientific analysis of the cause of this phenomenon, just as we can use the term 'water' and understand what it's like to get wet, without being aware of the chemical composition of water.

To get back to the mind/brain identity theory now, 'a thought about the weather' and 'a particular state of the brain' may be two ways of referring to precisely the same thing. The two phrases describe an identical event, but the meaning of the phrases is somewhat different. Most of us would use the mental description 'a thought about the weather' to describe this thing, but, according to the type-identity theory, a scientist could, in principle, give a detailed analysis of the brain state which is this thought. What is more, a type-identity theorist would argue that all thoughts of this type are actually brain states of this same type. One advantage of this theory of the mind is that it suggests the sorts of things which neuropsychologists could look for, namely the physical states of the brain which correspond to various thought types. However, there are several objections to the type-identity theory.

CRITICISMS OF TYPE-IDENTITY THEORY

NO KNOWLEDGE OF BRAIN PROCESSES

We have direct knowledge about our thoughts, yet most of us know nothing about brain processes. Some people see this as an objection to physicalism: thought cannot be the same as a brain process because it is possible to know about the thought without knowing anything about neurophysiology. We all of us have a privileged access to our own thoughts: that is, we know better than anyone else what our own conscious thoughts are; this is not so with brain states. Yet if thoughts and brain states are identical, they should share the same properties.

However, this objection is not a serious problem for the physicalist. We may not know anything about the chemical composition of water, yet this does not stop us understanding the concept 'water', and recognizing its taste when we drink it. Similarly all thoughts may be brain processes, yet there is no reason why thinkers should be expected to understand the precise nature of these brain processes in order to understand their thoughts.

PROPERTIES OF THOUGHTS AND OF BRAIN STATES

If a thought about my sister is identical with a certain brain state, then it follows that the thought must be located in exactly the same place as the brain state. But this seems a little strange: thoughts don't seem to have precise locations in this way. Yet it is a consequence of the type-identity theory that they should do. If I have a fluorescent green after-image from staring at a bright light, this after-image is a certain size, a lurid colour, and particular shape, yet my brain state is presumably very different in these respects. How then could the after-image be identical with a specific brain state?

ALL THOUGHTS ARE ABOUT SOMETHING

All thoughts are about something: it is impossible to have a thought about nothing at all. If I think 'Paris is my favourite city', then my thought is related to a place in the actual world. But brain processes and states do not seem to be about anything: they do not seem to relate to anything outside themselves in the way that thoughts do.

QUALIA: WHAT IT IS LIKE

Type physicalism, like many attempted solutions to the Mind/Body Problem, is often criticized for failing to take into account conscious experience: what it is actually like to be in a certain state. Consciousness may be hard to define, but it certainly includes sensations, feelings, pain, joy, desire, and so on. The Latin word *qualia* is sometimes used as a general term to cover such things. Although we can talk about 'water' and 'H_2O' as alternative descriptions of the same thing, 'a recollection of my first view of New York' cannot so easily be paraphrased as 'a certain brain state'. The difference is that in the second case we are not dealing with inanimate objects: there is a particular feel to this conscious experience. Yet to reduce this thought simply to a brain state gives no explanation of how this could possibly be so. It ignores one of the most basic phenomena associated with consciousness and thinking: the existence of *qualia*. To emphasize this point, consider the difference between the purely physical aspects of a terrible pain – in terms of the behaviour of nerve cells and so on – and the actual excruciating feeling of the pain: the physical description fails completely to catch what it is really like to experience this state.

INDIVIDUAL DIFFERENCES

Yet another criticism of the type-identity theory is that it insists that, for example, thoughts about the weather must all be brain states of the same type, even when the thoughts are had by different people. But there may be good reasons for believing that different people's brains function in slightly different ways, so that different brain states in different people could still give rise to a similar thought.

Even this presupposes that thoughts can be neatly divided up: that we can say where one thought ends and another begins. A basic assumption of the type-identity theory is that two people can have thoughts of precisely the same type. On closer analysis this seems to be a dubious assumption to make. If you and I are both thinking that the dark sky looks beautiful, we may express ourselves in identical words. We may both draw attention to the particular way the clouds are illuminated by the moon, and so on. But are we necessarily thinking a thought of the same type?

My thought about the beauty of the sky is not easily isolated from the whole of my experience of night-time skies, which is obviously very different from yours. Or again, if I believe that the author of *Nineteen Eighty-Four* wrote under a pseudonym, and you believe that Eric Blair wrote under a pseudonym, do we share a thought of the same type? Certainly our statements of our beliefs would refer to the same man, who was more usually known in literary circles as George Orwell. Yet there is no easy answer to such questions. What they show is the difficulty of carving up our mental life into neat slices which can then be removed and compared with slices from other people's mental lives. If it is impossible to determine when two people are having thoughts of the same type, then type-identity physicalism is implausible as a theory of the mind.

TOKEN-IDENTITY THEORY

One way round some of these criticisms of type-identity theory is provided by token-identity theory. Like type-identity theory, token-identity theory, which is another form of physicalism, states that all thoughts are identical with brain states. However, unlike type theory, token-identity theory allows that thoughts of the same type need not all be brain states of the same type. This theory uses the basic distinction between 'type' and 'token', a distinction that is most easily explained through examples. All copies of the book *War and Peace* are *tokens* of the particular *type* (the novel *War and Peace*); if you own a Volkswagen 'Beetle' car, you own a token of the particular type (a 'Beetle' car). The type is the species; the token is the individual instance of the species. What the token-identity theory says is that individual tokens of a particular type of thought are not necessarily physical states of precisely the same type.

So, when I think 'Bertrand Russell was a philosopher' today, this may involve a different brain state from when I thought that thought yesterday. Similarly, in order for you to think this thought, you needn't be in the same brain state as I was on either occasion.

The token–identity theory, however, is open to at least one major criticism.

CRITICISMS OF TOKEN-IDENTITY THEORY

SAME BRAIN STATES COULD BE DIFFERENT THOUGHTS

This simple token–identity theory would seem to allow that two people could be physically identical, right down to the very smallest molecule, and yet differ completely mentally. This seems to make the mental too much independent of the physical. It makes the relationship between the physical and the mental completely mysterious: more mysterious even than does mind/body dualism.

However, token–identity theorists usually build the notion of supervenience into their theory. A property of something is *supervenient* on another property (literally, 'goes above') if it depends on that other one for its existence. So, for instance, beauty (assuming it to be skin deep) can be said to supervene on physical attributes: if two people are physically identical, then it is impossible for one of them to be beautiful and the other not. However, this is not to say that all beautiful people are identical with each other; merely that if two people are identical cell for cell, one cannot be beautiful and the other not. If we adapt the token–identity theory of mind by adding to it the idea that mental properties are supervenient on physical ones, it means that if the physical properties are kept the same, the mental ones cannot vary. In other words, if two people are in precisely the same brain state, they will have the same mental experience. However, this does not mean that just because two people are having the same mental experience they must be having the same brain state.

BEHAVIOURISM

Behaviourism provides a rather different way out of the Mind/Body Problem from the dualist and physicalist theories we have examined. Behaviourists deny the existence of the mind altogether. Let us examine in more detail how they could plausibly deny what to most people seems to be obvious.

When we describe someone as being in pain, or as irritated, this is not, the behaviourist argues, a description of that person's mental experience. Rather it is a description of that person's public behaviour or potential behaviour in hypothetical situations. In other words it is a description of what they would do in such and such circumstances, that is, their dispositions to behave. To be in pain is to have a tendency to wince, groan, cry, scream, and so on, depending on the intensity of the pain. Being irritated is having a tendency to shout, stamp one's feet, and answer people rudely. Although we talk about our mental states, according to the behaviourist that is just a shorthand way of describing our behaviour and tendencies to behave in certain ways. This way of describing mental behaviour has led us to believe that the mind is a separate thing. Gilbert Ryle (1900–76), a famous behaviourist philosopher, called this dualistic view 'the dogma of the ghost in the machine', the ghost being the mind and the machine the body.

The behaviourist's account makes the Mind/Body Problem a pseudo-problem – not a genuine problem. There is no problem of explaining the relationship between mind and body because mental experience is easily accounted for in terms of behaviour patterns. So, rather than solving the problem, the behaviourists claim to have dissolved it completely.

CRITICISMS OF BEHAVIOURISM

PRETENDING

One criticism sometimes made of behaviourism is that it fails to make a distinction between someone actually being in pain and someone pretending to be in pain. If all talk of the mental is to be reduced to descriptions of behaviour, then there is no room for an explanation of the difference between a convincing actor and someone who is genuinely in agony.

Against this objection a behaviourist could point out that a dispositional analysis of someone pretending to be in pain would be different from that of someone actually in pain. Although their behaviour would be superficially similar, there would certainly be circumstances in which it would differ. For instance, someone pretending to be in pain is unlikely to be able to produce all the physiological accompaniments of pain – temperature changes, sweating, and the like. Also, someone who is pretending to be in pain would respond very differently to pain-killing drugs from someone who was genuinely in pain: the pretender would have no way of telling when the drugs had started to work, whereas the person who was actually in pain would realize because of a change in his or her pain behaviour.

QUALIA

Another criticism of behaviourism is that it fails to include any reference to what it actually feels like to be in a particular mental state. By reducing all mental events to behavioural tendencies, behaviourism leaves *qualia* out of the equation. It is surely a major criticism of the theory that it reduces the experience of actually being in pain to simply having a disposition to scream, wince, and say 'I am in pain'. There is something which it really feels like to be in pain, and this is an essential aspect of mental life, yet behaviourism ignores this.

HOW DO I LEARN ABOUT MY OWN BELIEFS?

According to behaviourism, the way that I learn about my own beliefs is precisely the same as the way that I learn about other people's beliefs, namely by observation of behaviour. But surely this is an inaccurate picture of what actually happens. It may be true that I can make interesting discoveries about what I actually believe by listening to what I say, and monitoring what I do in various circumstances. However, I do not need to make observations of my own behaviour in order to know such things as that I believe that murder is wrong, or that I live in England. I know these things without needing to act as a private detective investigating my own behaviour. So behaviourism does not give a satisfactory explanation of the difference between routes to self-knowledge and ways of finding out about other people's beliefs.

A possible reply to this criticism is that what I do when I introspect (look into myself), to see if I believe that, for instance, torture is cruel, is to think to myself 'What would I say and do if I learnt of someone being tortured?' The answer to that question would then reveal to me my relevant dispositions. If this is true, then the behaviourist is justified in assuming that there is no important difference between finding out about one's own case and finding out about someone else's. However, this analysis of introspection is not particularly convincing: it does not match with what I feel that I do when I introspect.

PAIN OF THE PARALYSED

Since behaviourism is based entirely upon the responses or potential responses of the individual in question, it seems to follow that on a behaviourist analysis people who are completely paralysed cannot have mental experience. If they cannot move, and never will be able to, how can they behave in any way? A behaviourist would have to say that the completely paralysed cannot feel pain, since they show no pain behaviour. And yet from the evidence of people who have been paralysed and regain movement we know that people who are paralysed often have very rich mental experience, and certainly have the capacity for experiencing pain.

BELIEFS CAN CAUSE BEHAVIOUR

A further criticism of behaviourism is that it does not allow the possibility that a person's beliefs could be a cause of their behaviour. On a behaviourist analysis, the cause of someone putting on their raincoat is not a belief that it is raining. Rather it is the tendency to put on a raincoat that is the main constituent of the belief. Mental events cannot cause behaviour because they do not exist independently of behaviour: according to behaviourism, mental events are just dispositions to behave in certain ways. Yet it is surely true that, at least on occasion, our mental events do lead to behaviour. I put on my coat *because* I think it's going to rain. But a behaviourist couldn't use my belief that it is going to rain even as an explanation of my behaviour because my belief is actually constituted by the behaviour, and by my disposition to behave in certain ways: the belief and the action are not separable.

FUNCTIONALISM

Functionalism is a recently developed approach to the Mind/Body Problem. It concentrates on the functional role of mental states: in practice this means concentrating on inputs, outputs, and the relation between inner states. A functionalist defines any mental state in terms of its typical relations to other mental states and its effects on behaviour. So a thought about the weather is defined in terms of its relations to other thoughts, and to behaviour: what leads me to have the thought; its relation to my other thoughts; and what it leads me to do. As such, functionalism benefits from some of the insights of behaviourism – such as that mental activity is usually intimately linked with behavioural dispositions – whilst allowing that mental events can actually be causes of behaviour.

Functionalism can be more easily understood through a comparison with the relationship between a computer and its program. When talking about computers it is convenient to make a distinction between hardware and software. The hardware of a computer is what it is actually made out of: transistors, circuits, silicon chips, screen, keyboard, and so on. The software, on the other hand, is the program, the system of operations which the hardware carries out. The software can usually be adapted for use in a number of different systems. The software is usually a complicated system of instructions to the computer hardware, which can be physically carried out in a number of different ways, but achieving the same result.

Functionalism as a theory of mind is concerned with the software of thought rather than the hardware. In this it resembles behaviourism. In contrast, physicalism is concerned to show the relation between certain bits of hardware – the human brain – and a particular software package – human thought. Functionalism is not a theory about the hardware of thought at all, although it is certainly compatible with various kinds of physicalism: it is neutral about what sorts of physical systems mental programs operate in. Its main concern is to specify the relations which hold between different sorts of thought and behaviour.

CRITICISM OF FUNCTIONALISM

QUALIA: COMPUTERS AND PEOPLE

Whilst functionalism is an extremely popular theory of the mind among philosophers, a frequent criticism of it is that it does not give an adequate account of conscious experience and sensations: what it is like to be in pain, to be happy, to be thinking about the weather, and so on.

A similar objection is often made against the view that computers can have minds. For instance, the contemporary philosopher John Searle has used a thought experiment to attempt to indicate the difference between a human being understanding a story and a computer 'understanding' one. Imagine that you are locked in a room. You do not understand Chinese. Through a letterbox in the door come various Chinese characters printed on bits of card. On a table in the room is a book and a pile of bits of card with other Chinese characters on them. Your task is to match the Chinese character on the piece of card which came through the letterbox with a Chinese character in the book. The book will then indicate another, different, Chinese character which is paired with it. You must take this other character from the pile of cards on the table and push it back out through the letterbox. From outside the room it appears that you are answering questions about a story in Chinese. The cards coming into the room are questions written in Chinese; those you push back out are your answers, also in Chinese. Even though you don't understand Chinese, from outside the room it appears that you understand the story and are giving intelligent answers to the questions you are being asked about it. Yet you do not have any experience of understanding the story: you are simply manipulating what to you are meaningless characters.

A so-called 'intelligent' computer program is in the same position as you in Searle's 'Chinese room' thought experiment. Like you, it just manipulates symbols without genuinely understanding what they refer to. Consequently, if we think of functionalism on the computer analogy suggested above, it cannot give us a complete picture of the mind. It does not capture genuine understanding, making it equivalent to manipulating symbols.

OTHER MINDS

We have now examined most of the major attempts to solve the Mind/Body Problem. As we have seen, no theory of the mind is entirely satisfactory. Let's turn now to another issue in the philosophy of mind, the so-called Problem of Other Minds. How do I know that other people think, feel, and are conscious in the way that I am? I know for certain when I am in pain, but how can I ever be sure that someone else is? In the way I live my life I assume that other people are sentient beings, capable of experiences very similar to my own. But can I know this for sure? For all I know, other people could all be highly sophisticated robots, or, as they are sometimes called, automata, programmed to respond as if they had an inner life, when in fact they do not.

Whilst this notion may seem close to a form of paranoia, it is a serious question to which philosophers have devoted a great deal of attention. A study of it reveals important differences between the way we come to learn about our own experience and the way we learn about other people's experience.

NOT A PROBLEM FOR BEHAVIOURISM

Before looking at the most common way of answering these doubts about other people's experience, it is worth pointing out that the problem of Other Minds does not arise for behaviourists. To a behaviourist it is clearly appropriate to attribute mental experience to others on the basis of their behaviour since that is what the mind is: tendencies to behave in certain ways in certain situations. This gives rise to the infamous behaviourist joke: two behaviourists have sex and afterwards one says to the other 'That was great for you; how was it for me?'

THE ARGUMENT FROM ANALOGY

The most obvious answer to the doubt that other people are conscious is the Argument from Analogy. As we saw in Chapter 1 when we examined the Design Argument for God's existence, an argument from analogy is based on a comparison between two quite similar things. If one thing is like another in some respects, it is assumed that it will be like it in others.

Other people resemble me in many important respects: we are all members of the same species, and consequently we have quite similar bodies; we also behave quite similarly. When I'm in extreme pain I scream, and so do most members of the human species when they are in situations in which I would expect them to be experiencing pain. The argument from analogy claims that the similarities in body and behaviour between my own case and those of other people are enough for me to infer that other people are genuinely conscious in the way that I am.

CRITICISMS OF THE ARGUMENT FROM ANALOGY

NOT A PROOF

The Argument from Analogy does not provide a conclusive proof that other people have minds. Arguments from analogy require a good deal of supporting evidence. But in the case of this argument from analogy there is only a single instance — myself — in which I have witnessed the connection between a certain sort of body and behaviour and a certain sort of consciousness.

Not only this, but there are many ways in which other people's bodies and behaviour differ from my own. These differences may be more important than the similarities: I could use an argument from analogy to demonstrate that the differences between my body and behaviour and other people's indicate a probable difference in types of mental experience between us. Besides, arguments from analogy, being inductive, can only give probable evidence for their conclusions: they can never prove anything conclusively. So, at the very best, such an argument could only show that other people almost certainly do have minds. It's not a deductive proof, but, as we have seen in the chapter on science, there is no proof that the sun will rise tomorrow, yet we still have good grounds for feeling sure that it will.

UNVERIFIABLE

Yet there does not seem to be any way of showing conclusively that a statement such as 'he is in pain' is true, or, for that matter, that it is false. Just because someone is screaming, it does not follow that they are experiencing the same sort of thing as I do when I am in extreme pain. They may not be having any experience at all. Any verbal report of their experience is unreliable: a robot could have been programmed to answer persuasively in such circumstances. There is no possible observation which could confirm or refute the idea that that person is experiencing pain. Obviously the fact that someone was screaming would be enough in actual cases for us to be fairly certain that that person was in pain. But, from a logical point of view, the behaviour does not give absolute proof of pain (though most people work on the assumption that it *is* reliable).

Of course we may find it rather far-fetched to suppose that other people are not conscious. So we might be so sure already that other people do have minds that we would not need a conclusive proof of this matter – certainly most of us act on the assumption that they do, most of the time. Solipsism, as we saw in Chapter 5, is not a tenable position.

CONCLUSION

This chapter has concentrated on debate about dualism, physicalism, and the Problem of Other Minds. These are central issues in the philosophy of mind. Since philosophy is very much concerned with the nature of thought, many philosophers, particularly those who specialize in the philosophy of mind, have seen the sorts of questions discussed in this chapter as lying at the heart of almost every philosophical question. Certainly many of the most brilliant philosophers of the twentieth century focused their energies on questions in the philosophy of mind. As a result, much writing on this area is of a highly sophisticated and technical kind. The books listed below should give you some guidance through the complicated maze of writing on the subject.

FURTHER READING

An entertaining and accessible overview of many of the most important topics in this area is David Papineau's *Introducing Consciousness*, illustrated by Howard Selina (Cambridge: Icon Books, 2000). Two more conventional introductions covering many of the same issues in more detail are Robert Kirk's *Mind and Body* (Chesham: Acumen, 2003) and George Graham's *Philosophy of Mind: An Introduction* (2nd edition, Oxford: Blackwell, 1998). Tim Crane's *Mechanical Mind* (2nd edition, London: Routledge, 2003) approaches central questions within the philosophy of mind through the issue of whether the mind is like a computer.

The Mind's I, edited by Douglas R. Hofstadter and Daniel C. Dennett (London: Penguin, 1982), is an interesting and entertaining collection of articles, meditations, and short stories which deal with philosophical ideas about the mind. It includes John Searle's article 'Minds, Brains, and Programs', where he discusses the question of whether computers can really think. *Modern Philosophy of Mind*, edited by William Lyons (London: J. M. Dent, Everyman, 1995), is another very useful anthology of readings.

There are numerous online philosophy of mind resources. One very useful site is run by the philosopher David Chalmers and includes his annotated bibliography of contemporary work in the philosophy of mind. It is at www.u.arizona.edu/chalmers.

8

ART

Most people who visit art galleries, read novels and poetry, watch plays or ballet, go to see films, or listen to music have at some time wondered what art is. This is the basic question underlying all philosophy of art. This chapter considers several answers which have been given to it. It also examines a number of philosophical questions about the nature of art criticism.

The fact that new art forms such as film and photography have emerged and that art galleries have exhibited such things as a pile of bricks or a stack of cardboard boxes has forced us to think about the limits of what we are prepared to call art. Obviously art has meant different things to different cultures at different times: it has served ritualistic, religious, and entertainment purposes as well as embodying the beliefs, fears, and desires most central to the culture in which it was produced. In earlier times what counted as art seemed to be more clearly defined. Yet we now seem to have reached a stage when anything whatsoever can be a work of art. If this is so, what is it that makes one object or piece of writing or music rather than another worthy of being called art?

CAN ART BE DEFINED?

There is an immense variety among works of art: paintings, plays, films, novels, pieces of music, and dance may seem to have very little in common. This has led some philosophers to argue that art cannot be defined at all. They claim that it is a complete mistake to look for a common denominator since there is just too much variety among works of art for a definition which applies to them all to be satisfactory. To back this up they use the idea of a family resemblance, a notion used by the philosopher Ludwig Wittgenstein in his *Philosophical Investigations*.

THE FAMILY RESEMBLANCE VIEW

You may look a little like your father, and your father may resemble his sister. However, it is possible that you look nothing like your father's sister. In other words there may be overlapping resemblances between different members of a family without there being any one observable feature which they all share. Similarly, many games resemble each other, but it is difficult to see what solitaire, chess, rugby, and tiddlywinks have in common.

The resemblances between different sorts of art may be of this type: despite the obvious similarities between some works of art, there may be no observable features which they all share, no common denominators. If this is so, it is a mistake to look for any general definition of art. The best that we can hope for is a definition of an art form, such as the novel, the fiction film, or the symphony.

CRITICISMS OF THE FAMILY RESEMBLANCE VIEW

One way of proving this view false would be to produce a satisfactory definition of art. We will look at a number of attempts to do this below. However, it is worth noting that even in the case of family resemblances there is something which all members of a family do have in common: the fact that they are genetically related. And all games resemble each other in that they have the potential to be of absorbing non-practical interest to players or spectators. Now, whilst this definition of games is rather vague, and not entirely satisfactory – it doesn't, for example, help us to distinguish games from such activities as kissing or listening to music – it suggests that a more detailed and plausible definition could be found. If this can be done for games, there is no reason to rule out in advance the possibility of doing it for works of art. Of course, the common denominator of all works of art may turn out not to be particularly interesting or important, but it clearly might be possible to find one. Let us, then, consider some of the attempted definitions of art. We will examine the significant form, the idealist, and the institutional theories of art.

THE SIGNIFICANT FORM THEORY

The significant form theory, popular in the early part of the twentieth century and particularly linked with the art critic Clive Bell (1881–1964) and his book *Art*, begins with the assumption that all genuine works of art produce an aesthetic emotion in the spectator, listener, or reader. This emotion is different from the emotions of everyday life: it is distinctive in having nothing to do with practical concerns.

What is it about works of art that causes people to respond to them in this way? Why do works of art evoke this aesthetic emotion? The answer Bell gave is that all genuine works of art share a quality known as 'significant form', a term he coined. Significant form is a certain relation between parts – the distinctive features of a work of art's structure rather than of its subject matter. Although this theory is usually only applied to the visual arts it can equally well be taken as a definition of all of the arts.

So, for example, a significant form theorist considering what it is that makes Van Gogh's painting of a pair of old boots a work of art would point to the combination of colours and textures that possess significant form and therefore produce the aesthetic emotion in sensitive critics.

Significant form is an indefinable property that sensitive critics can intuitively recognize in a work of art. Unfortunately, insensitive critics are unable to appreciate significant form. Bell, unlike for instance the institutional theorists discussed below, believed art to be an evaluative concept: this means that to call something a work of art is not just to classify it, but also to say that it has a certain worth. All genuine works of art, of all ages and of all cultures, possess significant form.

CRITICISMS OF THE SIGNIFICANT FORM THEORY

CIRCULARITY

The argument for the significant form theory appears to be circular in that two of its key concepts are defined each in terms of the other. Significant form is simply those formal properties of a work which give rise to the aesthetic emotion. But the aesthetic emotion can only be understood as the emotion felt in the presence of significant form. This is unsatisfactory. If we cannot escape this circularity of definition, then the theory will remain spectacularly uninformative. We need some independent way of recognizing either significant form or else the aesthetic emotion. Without such an independent criterion of one or the other, the theory has a viciously circular definition at its heart. It is like looking up the word 'yes' in a dictionary to find it defined as 'the opposite of "no"'; and then looking up 'no' to find it defined as 'the opposite of "yes"'.

IRREFUTABILITY

A further objection to the theory is that it cannot be refuted. An assumption of the significant form theory is that there is just one emotion which all genuine experiencers of art feel when appreciating true works of art. However, this is extremely difficult, if not impossible, to prove.

If someone claims fully to have experienced a work of art but hasn't experienced this aesthetic emotion, then Bell would say that that person was mistaken: they either hadn't fully experienced it, or else were not a sensitive critic. But this is to assume what the theory is supposed to be proving: that there is indeed one aesthetic emotion and that it is produced by genuine works of art. The theory, then, appears irrefutable. And many philosophers believe that if a theory is logically impossible to refute because every possible observation would confirm it, then it is a meaningless theory.

Similarly, if we point to something which we consider to be a work of art and yet which doesn't evoke the aesthetic emotion in a sensitive critic, then a significant form theorist will claim that it is not a genuine work of art. Again, there is no possible observation which could prove such a person wrong in this.

THE IDEALIST THEORY

The idealist theory of art, given its most persuasive formulation by R. G. Collingwood (1889–1943) in his *The Principles of Art*, differs from other theories of art in that it holds that the actual work of art is non-physical: it is an idea or emotion in the artist's mind. This idea is given physical imaginative expression, and is modified through the artist's involvement with a particular artistic medium, but the artwork itself remains in the artist's mind. In some versions of the idealist theory great stress is put on the emotion expressed being a sincere one. This builds a strong evaluative element into the theory.

The idealist theory distinguishes art from craft. Works of art serve no particular purpose. They are created through the artist's involvement with a particular medium, such as oil paint or words. In contrast, craft objects are created for a particular purpose, and the craftsperson begins with a plan rather than designing the object in the process of making it. So, for example, a painting by Picasso serves no particular purpose, and was, presumably, not fully planned in advance, whereas the table at which I am sitting serves a very obvious function and was made according to a pre-existing design, a blueprint. The painting is a work of art; the table a work of craft. This is not to say that works of art cannot contain elements of craft: clearly many great works of art do contain such craft elements. Collingwood explicitly states that the two categories art and craft are not mutually exclusive. Rather, no work of art is solely a means to an end.

The idealist theory contrasts genuine works of art with mere entertainment art (art made with the purpose simply of entertaining people, or of arousing particular emotions). Genuine art has no purpose: it is an end in itself. Entertainment art is a craft, and therefore inferior to art proper. Similarly, purely religious art, so called, is considered to be craft because it was made for a specific purpose.

CRITICISMS OF THE IDEALIST THEORY

STRANGENESS

The main objection to the idealist theory is the strangeness of considering artworks to be ideas in the mind rather than physical objects. This means that when we go to an art gallery, all we are seeing is traces of the artists' actual creations. This is a difficult view to accept, though it is more plausible in the cases of literary and musical works of art where there is no single physical object that we can call the work of art.

TOO NARROW

A second objection to this theory is that it is too narrow: it seems to categorize many established works of art as only works of craft, not of art proper. Many great portrait paintings were painted in order to have a record of their sitter's appearance; many great plays written in order to entertain. Does this mean that because they were created with a specific purpose in mind they cannot be works of art? And what about architecture, which is traditionally one of the Fine Arts: most buildings are created for a specific purpose, so cannot be considered works of art on this theory.

THE INSTITUTIONAL THEORY

The so-called institutional theory of art is a recent attempt by such writers as the contemporary philosopher George Dickie (1936–) to explain how such varied pieces as the play *Macbeth*, Beethoven's Fifth Symphony, a pile of bricks, a urinal labelled 'Fountain', T. S. Eliot's poem *The Waste Land*, Swift's *Gulliver's Travels*, and William Klein's photographs can all be considered works of art. The theory states that there are two things that all these have in common.

First, they are all artefacts: that is, they have all been worked on to some extent by human beings. 'Artefact' is used in quite a loose way – even a piece of driftwood picked up on the seashore could be considered an artefact if someone displayed it in an art gallery. Placing it in a gallery in order to get people to look at it in a certain way would count as working on it. In fact this definition of an artefact is so loose as to add nothing important to the concept of art.

Second, and more importantly, they have all been given the status of a work of art by some member or members of the art world such as a gallery owner, a publisher, a producer, a conductor, or an artist. In every case someone with the appropriate authority has done the equivalent of christening them as works of art. He or she has conferred upon the artefact the status of 'candidate for appreciation'.

This may sound as if it means that works or art are simply those things which certain people call works of art, an apparently circular claim. In fact it is not very far from this. However, the members of the art world need not actually go through any sort of ceremony of naming something a work of art, they need not even actually call it a work of art: it is enough that they treat the work as art. The institutional theory, then, says that some individuals and groups in our society have an ability to change any artefact into a work of art by a simple action of 'christening', which may take the form of calling something 'art', but more often amounts to publishing, exhibiting, or performing the work. Artists themselves can be members of this art world. All members of this elite have the equivalent of King Midas's ability to turn everything he touched to gold.

CRITICISMS OF THE INSTITUTIONAL THEORY

DOESN'T DISTINGUISH GOOD FROM BAD ART

It is sometimes argued that the institutional theory is a poor theory of art because it seems to justify the most pretentious and the most superficial objects being considered works of art. If I were a member of the art world I could, by exhibiting it in a gallery, make my left shoe into a work of art.

It is certainly true that the institutional theory does allow that almost anything could become a work of art. Christening something a work of art does not mean that it is a *good* work of art, nor for that matter a *bad* one. It only makes the object a work of art in the classificatory sense: in other words it puts it into the class of things we call works of art. This differs from the way we often use the word 'art' not just to classify something, but often also to suggest that it is good of its kind. Sometimes too we use the term metaphorically to talk about things which are not literally works of art at all, for instance when we say such things as 'that omelette is a work of art'. The institutional theory has nothing to tell us about either of these evaluative uses of the word 'art'. It is a theory about what all works of art – good, bad, and indifferent – have in common. It is only about the classificatory sense of 'art'. In this sense, then, the image of members of the art world having the Midas touch is inappropriate. Gold is valuable; but, according to the institutional theory, there need be nothing of any value whatsoever in a work of art.

However, most people who ask the question 'What is art?' are not just interested in what we call art, but want to know why we value some objects above others. Both the significant form and idealist theories are partly evaluative: according to them, to call something a work of art is to say that it is good in some sense, either because it has significant form or because it is a sincere artistic expression of an emotion. The institutional theory, however, does not attempt to give an answer to evaluative questions about art. It is extremely open about what can be counted as art. Some see this as its greatest virtue; others as its most serious defect.

CIRCULARITY

Many people have thought the institutional theory to be circular. At its crudest the theory seems to say that whatever a certain group of people – the art world – choose to call art is art. What makes these people members of this group is that they have the capacity to confer this status. 'Work of art' and 'member of the art world' have been defined each in terms of the other.

However, a defender of the institutional theory will point out that, although perhaps circular in some sense, the theory is not *viciously* circular. The theory is not as uninformative as the summary in the previous paragraph might suggest. Defenders of the institutional theory have a great deal to say about the nature of the art world, its history, and its various ways of operating. Nevertheless, the theory does seem less informative than most. This is partly because it does not provide any explanation of why a member of the art world might choose to confer the status of work of art on one artefact rather than another.

WHAT CRITERIA DOES THE ART WORLD USE?

Perhaps the most telling objection to the institutional theory is one that has been made by the contemporary philosopher and writer on art, Richard Wollheim (1923–2003): even if we agree that members of the art world have the power to make any artefacts works of art, they must have reasons for making some artefacts art and not others. If they don't have any logic behind what they do, then why should the category of art have any interest for us? And if they do have reasons, then these are what determine whether or not something is art. Analysis of these reasons would be far more interesting and informative than the rather empty institutional theory. If we could identify these reasons, then the institutional theory would be unnecessary.

However, the institutional theory at least reminds us that what makes something a work of art is a cultural matter, dependent on social institutions at particular times rather than on some timeless canon. Recent theorizing about the definition of art has tended to put stress on the historical aspects.

ART AND EVOLUTION

Some philosophers have started to take a longer historical perspective when addressing questions about what art is. Looking back to the Pleistocene period, the longest period of human evolution, they maintain that art arises from instincts and that its biological origins shed light on what it is and why it is so important to all human cultures. Denis Dutton (1944–2010), for instance, has written about an 'art instinct', a universal phenomenon that explains why, for example, there is a widespread appreciation of landscape paintings that show rolling hills, water, and trees: this is because the depicted environment is one that would have been hospitable for early humans. The idea is that a preference for such scenes in real life would have led to a greater chance of survival, and that over the long period of human evolution in the Pleistocene, humans evolved to prefer such scenes.

Evolutionary theory can also give an explanation of why artists and works of art are so highly prized despite being of no practical use. They are like the male peacock's tail – flamboyant display gestures that indicate that their possessors/creators have a surplus of energy and prowess. The male peacock's huge and beautiful tail is a burden to it, making it easier for predators to catch, but at the same time it signals to potential mates how healthy and fit it is. Similarly, creating works of art serves no immediate practical purpose, but those who do create them signal their virtuosity and skill. Like the peacocks with their elaborate tails, artists have an advantage in terms of sexual selection, even though their activity does not appear to have practical use.

CRITICISM OF EVOLUTIONARY ART THEORY

ALTERNATIVE EXPLANATIONS

While it is plausible that there is some biological explanation for the universality of art across a wide range of cultures, there are numerous alternative explanations of the actual process of genetic selection that are just as plausible as the ones suggested above. For example, take the question of why so many people find landscapes with rolling hills, trees, and water in them attractive. This might be because they are hospitable environments, but it might equally be because the shape of the rolling hills triggers recognition of the contours of the mother's breast. Perhaps the instinctive (or learned) recognition that feeding is associated with the curves of the breast may carry over to the way we appreciate curves in landscape. There is no straightforward test to decide between these and other competing accounts of how we came to have the particular instincts that we do. This is not to deny the genetic component in our appreciation of art, only to question the particular accounts that are given of how this came to be so.

ART CRITICISM

Another important area of philosophical debate about the arts has focused on the methods and justifications of various kinds of writing about art. One of the central debates in this area has been about the extent to which an artist's stated intentions are relevant to critical interpretation of a work of art.

ANTI-INTENTIONALISM

Anti-intentionalists argue that we must pay attention only to intentions embodied in the work of art itself. Anything gleaned from diaries, interviews with the artist, artistic manifestos, and so on, is not directly relevant to the act of genuine critical interpretation. Such information is more relevant to a study of the artist's psychology. Psychology is an interesting subject in itself, and it can tell us much about the origins of works of art. But the origin of a work should not be confused with its meaning. Criticism should deal only with evidence *internal* to the work (i.e. contained within it). Personal statements about what the artist had in mind are *external* to the work, and so irrelevant to genuine criticism. Anti-intentionalists, such as the critics William Wimsatt (1907–75) and Monroe Beardsley (1915–80), writing in the 1940s, call the supposed mistake of relying on external evidence the Intentional Fallacy.

This anti-intentionalist view is used to defend close readings of literary texts and close analyses of other artworks. It is based on the idea that works of art are public in some sense, and that once they have created them the artists should have no more control over their interpretation than anyone else.

A similar claim has been made more recently, in metaphorical terms, by those, such as Roland Barthes (1915–80), who have declared the death of the author. Part of what they mean by this is that once a literary text is made public, it is for the reader to interpret it: the author should no longer be considered to hold a privileged position in this respect. A consequence of this view is that texts are considered more important than the authors who produce them, and the role of the critic is upgraded. The meaning of texts is created by the reader's interpretation rather than the writer's intentions. The anti-intentionalist view is, then, a claim about which aspects of a work are relevant to the critic's assessment of it.

CRITICISMS OF ANTI-INTENTIONALISM

MISTAKEN VIEW OF INTENTION

One criticism of the anti-intentionalist's position is that it rests on a mistaken view of what intentions are. It treats intentions as if they were always mental events which occur just before we do anything. In fact many philosophers believe that intentions are typically involved in the way we do things: they are not so easily separated from the actions themselves. So when I intentionally turn on the light I do not have to have a mental event just prior to reaching for the switch: it can occur at the same time as I reach for the switch, and the very act of reaching for the switch embodies the intention.

However, this is not really a satisfactory argument against anti-intentionalism since what the anti-intentionalists object to is not simply basing criticism on intentions, but rather basing it on anything *external* to the work of art. Anti-intentionalists are happy to treat intentions that are actually embodied in the work as relevant to criticism.

IRONY

Another, more telling objection to anti-intentionalism is that certain sorts of artistic device, such as irony, require an appreciation of an artist's intentions. In many cases these will be intentions of an external kind.

Irony is saying or depicting one thing, but meaning its opposite. For instance, when a friend says 'It's a lovely day', it may not be obvious whether this is meant literally or ironically. One way of deciding would be to look at such things as the context in which it was said – was it pouring with rain, for instance? Another would be to pay attention to the tone of voice in which it was said. But if neither of these pieces of evidence decided the issue, an obvious way of finding out would be to ask the speaker whether it was meant ironically: in other words to appeal to intentions of the external kind.

In some uses of irony in art, evidence external to the work can be extremely useful in deciding the meaning. It seems unreasonable to dismiss completely this source of information about the work. An anti-intentionalist would probably reply to this that if the irony is not readily understandable from a close analysis of the work, then it is not relevant to criticism since criticism deals with what is public. Any irony which relies on the external intentions of the artist is too much like a secret code to matter very much.

TOO NARROW A VIEW OF ART CRITICISM

A third objection to anti-intentionalism is that it takes too narrow a view of what art criticism is. Good art criticism will make use of any available evidence, be it internal or external to the work in question. It is excessively restricting to the critic to lay down hard-and-fast rules in advance about what sorts of evidence may be used to back up critical comments.

PERFORMANCE, INTERPRETATION, AUTHENTICITY

Performance of works of art may raise philosophical difficulties in some ways similar to those involved in the practice of art criticism. Every performance is an interpretation of that work. There are particular difficulties which arise when the work of art is from a much earlier period. Here I will consider the case of the performance of music of previous centuries as an example of this, but similar arguments can be used about, for example, historically accurate performances of Shakespeare's plays.

HISTORICAL AUTHENTICITY IN PERFORMANCE

In recent years there has been a great increase in the number of concerts and recordings in which musicians have been attempting to produce historically authentic sounds. This usually means playing on the kind of instruments available at the time the music was written rather than on their modern descendants. So, for example, an orchestra attempting to give a historically authentic performance of Bach's 'Brandenburg Concertos' would shun modern instruments, and would play instead the sorts of instruments available in Bach's day with their characteristic sounds and limitations. The conductor would consult as much historical research as possible to discover the tempo and style of interpretation typical in Bach's day. The aim of such a performance would be to reproduce as closely as possible the sounds which Bach's first audiences would have heard.

Whilst such performances are clearly of great interest to a historian of music, they raise a number of important philosophical questions about the status of different performances of a work of art. Using the word 'authentic' to describe these performances suggests that performances on modern-day instruments are somehow inauthentic: it implies that there is something significantly better about the 'authentic' performances. This raises the question of whether musical performances ought to aim at this kind of historical authenticity. There are a number of objections to the view that they should.

CRITICISMS OF HISTORICAL AUTHENTICITY IN PERFORMANCE

TIME-TRAVEL FANTASY

One criticism of the authentic performance movement is that a historically authentic performance can never be achieved. What motivates it is a naive attempt to travel back in time to hear the sounds which the composer would have heard. But what the 'authentic' performers forget is that, whilst we can successfully recreate the instruments of a former age, we can never simply blot out the music which has been composed and played since that time. In other words, we can never hear the music with historically authentic ears. Listening to Bach today we are aware of the major developments in music since his day; we are familiar with the sounds of modern instruments played with modern techniques. We have heard atonal music and know the sound of the modern piano better than we do the harpsichord. Consequently Bach's music has a completely different significance for the present-day listener than it did for its original audiences.

SIMPLISTIC VIEW OF MUSICAL INTERPRETATION

Another criticism of this striving after a historically authentic performance is that it involves a simplistic view of musical interpretation. It makes the judgement of whether or not a particular performance is a good one dependent solely on historical rather than on other relevant artistic considerations. It severely limits the performer's scope for creative interpretation of a score. It creates a museum of musical performance rather than allowing the performers of each new generation the possibility of a fresh and challenging interpretation of the composer's work, one which takes into account both the history of music and the history of interpretation of that particular piece.

HISTORICAL INTERPRETATIONS CAN MISS THE SPIRIT

An exaggerated concern for historical accuracy can often detract from the interpretation of a piece of music. A performer whose main concern is history may well fail to do the composer's work justice: there is much to be said for a sensitive interpretation which aims to capture the spirit of the composer's work rather than to reproduce the original sounds. This is a different sort of authenticity: it is an authenticity of interpretation, using 'authenticity' to mean something like 'artistic sincerity', rather than simply historical accuracy.

FORGERIES AND ARTISTIC VALUE

Another question about authenticity which raises philosophical issues is that of whether an original painting is of any greater artistic value than a perfect forgery. Here I will just consider forgeries of paintings, but there can be forgeries of any type of artwork that is a physical object: for instance, a sculpture, a print, a photograph, and so on. Copies of novels, poems, and symphonies are not thought of as forgeries. However, original manuscripts can be forged, and imitations written in the style of a particular author or composer can be passed off as genuine.

To begin with, it is important to distinguish between different types of forgery. The two basic types are the perfect copy, and the painting in the style of a famous artist. An exact copy of the *Mona Lisa* would be a forgery of the first type; the forger Van Meegeren's paintings in the style of Vermeer, which in fact fooled most of the experts, are examples of the second type – there was no original from which they were copied. Obviously only the actual manuscript of a play, novel, or poem could be faked in the first sense. However, forgeries of the second type, for example of Shakespeare's plays, could be made by someone cleverly imitating a writer's style.

Should forgeries be treated as significant works of art in their own right? If the forger is capable of producing work which convinces experts that it is by the original artist, then surely the forger is as skilled as the original artist and should be treated as that artist's equal. There are arguments both for and against this position.

PRICE, SNOBBERY, RELICS

Perhaps it is only the financial concerns of the art world, the obsession with how much a painting is worth, which makes people prize originals over good fakes. If there is only a single copy of each painting then the art auctioneers can sell each painting for a very high price as a unique object. This is sometimes known as the 'Sotheby's Effect', after the famous art auctioneers. If there are many copies of a painting, then the price of each copy is likely to drop, especially if the original is not considered any different in status from the copies. This would in effect put paintings in the same position as prints.

Or else perhaps it is not just the financial aspect of the art world but also the snobbery of art collectors which leads to the emphasis on original paintings rather than copies. Collectors enjoy owning a unique object: for them it may be more important to own an original sketch by Constable than to own a perfect copy of it, simply as a matter of snob, rather than artistic, value.

Another motivation for owning originals is to do with their appeal as relics. Relics are fascinating because of their history: a piece of the True Cross (the cross on which Christ was crucified) would have a special fascination compared with other indistinguishable bits of wood simply because it is believed to have been in direct contact with Christ's flesh. Similarly an original Van Gogh painting may be prized because this was an object which the great painter touched, paid attention to, put his artistic effort into, and so on.

Price, snob value, and value as relic have little to do with artistic merit. The first is to do with rarity, the fluctuations of collectors' tastes, and the manipulations of the art dealers; the second is a matter of social rivalry; the third is psychological, to do with the way we treat objects. If these three factors explain the causes of the widespread preference for original works of art over good forgeries, then perhaps good forgeries are really just as *artistically* significant as originals. However, there are several strong arguments against such a view.

PERFECT FAKES

One reason to prefer originals to fakes is that we can never be certain that a fake is really a perfect one. Just because a forgery of a Van Gogh painting is good enough to fool the experts now, it does not mean that it will fool future experts. If differences can become visible at a later stage, then we can never be sure that a fake is a perfect one. So, even if we believed that a perfect fake would be of equal artistic merit to the original, in any actual instance of a fake we will never be certain that the fake is really an accurate copy.

Against this view it is worth pointing out that the kinds of difference between fake and original which are likely to emerge will usually be very minor. It is implausible to suppose that they will very often be of a kind to alter substantially our views of the painting's artistic worth.

WORKS OF ART VERSUS ARTISTS

Even if someone managed to produce a painting which couldn't be told apart from one by, say, Cézanne, this is a very different achievement from that of Cézanne himself. Part of what we value about Cézanne's achievement is not simply the production of an isolated beautiful painting, but rather the way in which he created an original style and a whole range of paintings. His originality is part of his achievement, as is the way the different paintings he produced over his lifetime contribute to our understanding of each individual image he made. We can only fully appreciate his artistic achievement if we can place each painting in the context of his entire output.

Now, whilst a forger may have the mechanical skills as a painter that Cézanne had, Cézanne's achievement should not be reduced to his skill as a craftsperson. The forger in his slavish copying can never hope to be a great painter, because the forger cannot be original in the way that Cézanne was.

In the case of a forger producing works in the style of Cézanne (forgeries of the second type) rather than actual copies of real paintings, there might be more grounds for comparing the forgeries' artistic merit with that of Cézanne's paintings. But even in such a case the forger would be copying a style rather than creating it, and we tend to value the creativity of the original artist over the skill of an imitator. Creativity is an important aspect of artistic merit.

What this shows is that we certainly should not consider the forger as the equal of the original artist just because he or she is capable of producing a convincing forgery. But even so, with the case of a copy of an original painting, we could still appreciate Cézanne's artistic merit through looking at the copy. So this is not an argument against the artistic value of forgeries but against the artistic merit of forgers. The copy would allow us to see evidence of Cézanne's genius, not the forger's.

THE MORAL ARGUMENT

What is really wrong with forgeries is that by their nature they involve an attempt to deceive viewers about their origins. A forgery would not be a forgery without the intent to deceive: it would be a copy, or an experiment in painting in the style of another artist – what is known as pastiche. It is partly because of the deception involved – the equivalent of telling a lie – that forgeries are inferior to originals. However, there may be good reasons for keeping some moral and artistic questions separate: even if a brilliant forgery involves deception, it may nevertheless still be impressive as a work of art.

CONCLUSION

In this chapter I have considered a variety of philosophical questions about art and art criticism, ranging from questions about the definition of what art is to questions about the aesthetic status of forgeries. Much talk about art by artists, critics, and interested spectators is confused and illogical. Employing philosophical rigour and insisting on clarity of argument in this area can only improve matters. As in all areas of philosophy there is no guarantee that clear argument will provide convincing answers to the difficult questions, but it does increase the chances of this happening.

FURTHER READING

Three useful general introductions to the philosophy of art are Colin Lyas's *Aesthetics* (London: Routledge, 1997), Noël Carroll's *Philosophy of Art: A Contemporary Introduction* (London: Routledge, 1999), and Gordon Graham's *Philosophy of the Arts: An Introduction to Aesthetics* (2nd edition, London: Routledge, 2000). My own book, *The Art Question* (London: Routledge, 2003), focuses on the definition of art. Matthew Kieran's *Revealing Art: Why Art Matters* (London: Routledge, 2004) is accessible and interesting. A thorough reference book in this area with detailed suggestions for further reading is *The Oxford Handbook of Aesthetics*, edited by Jerrold Levinson (Oxford: Oxford University Press, 2003). Denis Dutton's *The Art Instinct* (Oxford: Oxford University Press, 2009) is a lively and readable attempt to demonstrate the biological origins of a universal art instinct.

Arguing About Art, edited by Alex Neill and Aaron Ridley (3rd edition, London: Routledge, 2007), is a good collection of articles on contemporary issues in the philosophy of art. They have also edited a more comprehensive anthology of writing in this area, *The Philosophy of Art: Readings Ancient and Modern* (New York: McGraw-Hill, 1995). Another useful anthology of readings in the philosophy of art is *Aesthetics: A Comprehensive Anthology*, edited by Steven M. Cahn and Aaron Meskin (Oxford: Wiley-Blackwell, 2007).

Terry Eagleton's *Literary Theory: An Introduction* (Oxford: Blackwell, 1983) provides an interesting survey of some of the developments in the philosophy of literature, although his emphasis is on the continental rather than the Anglo-American tradition of theory.

On the topic of authenticity in early music *Authenticity and Early Music*, edited by Nicholas Kenyon (Oxford: Oxford University Press, 1988), is very good. Denis Dutton's *The Forger's Art* (Berkeley, Calif.: University of California Press, 1983) is a fascinating collection of articles on the status of forgeries.

INDEX